Complete Guide to Sea Fishing

By the same Author

SEA FISHING IN CORNWALL

SEA FISHING IN SOUTH DEVON

SEA FISHING IN DORSET

SEA FISHING IN HAMPSHIRE AND THE ISLE OF WIGHT

SEA FISHING IN SUSSEX

SEA FISHING IN NORTH DEVON AND SOMERSET

SEA FISHING IN KENT

THE MODERN SEA ANGLER

THE SEASIDE POCKET COMPANION

SPINNING AND TROLLING FOR SEA FISH

FISHING FOR BASS (*Illustrated by* Arnold Wiles)

SEA ANGLING HOTSPOTS

Complete Guide to Sea Fishing

By
HUGH STOKER

ERNEST BENN LIMITED
LONDON & TONBRIDGE

Published by Ernest Benn Limited
25 New Street Square, Fleet Street, London, EC4A 3JA
Third impression (revised) 1968
Fourth impression (revised) 1974
© Hugh Stoker 1968
Printed in Great Britain
ISBN 0 510–22501–2

Tackle drawings by the author
with fish drawings by R. E. Legge

Contents

1	Choosing the Right Tackle	7
2	Pier, Harbour Wall and Rock Fishing	22
3	Beach Fishing	33
4	Spinning	43
5	Sea Fishing with Freshwater Tackle	53
6	Prelude to Boat Fishing	58
7	Boat Fishing at Anchor	70
8	Boat Fishing under Way	76
9	Sea Fish A.B.C.	86
10	Baits	138

List of Illustrations

1	Centre Pin Reel	12
2	Multiplier Reel	13
3	Fixed and Spool Reel	14
4	Sea Leads	18
5 and 6	Swivel Links and Sea Hooks	20
7	Drop-net	23
8	Sliding Float Tackle	24
9	Paternoster	28
10 and 11	Paternoster-trot and Free-running leger	29
12	Wessex Leger	30
13 and 14	Sunken Float Tackles	31
15	Sandbag Sinker	37
16	Bubble Floats	44
17 and 18	Anti-kink Leads	46 and 47
19	Spoons	49
20	Spinning from well above water level	51
21	Making a small spiked lead	55
22	Two types of Anchor	63
23	Plummet for taking samples of sea-bed	66
24	Types of Wreck Buoys	67
25	Driftline with automatic lead release	73
26	Trolling Tackle	78
27	Baited spoon tackle for bass	79
28 and 28a	Rod Rest for Dinghy	81
29	Checking a Drifting Boat	83
	Sea Fish	86 to 137
30 and 31	Trolling over tide-swept shoals	90
32	Cuddy Fly	94
33	Tackle for 'above the rocks' conger fishing	102
34	Float tackle for mullet	116
35	The Greater Weaver, showing venomous spines	133
36	Hook set-up for trolling with fish-strips	145
37	Method of opening mussels	147
38	Sandeel rake	155

CHAPTER 1

Choosing the Right Tackle

THE first and most important step towards becoming a successful sea angler is to select a properly balanced outfit of tackle. It might be a good idea, therefore, to begin this book on sea fishing by discussing some of the problems which confront the novice when choosing his first rod and reel, and to point out various ways in which he can avoid wasting money on unsuitable tackle.

RODS

Glass-fibre is undoubtedly the most suitable material for all kinds of sea angling rods. For sheer strength, flexibility and durability it has no equal, and unlike the built-cane and greenheart rods used by earlier generations of sea fishermen, glass-fibre is impervious to water, and cannot rot, warp or take on a 'set'.

There are two sorts of glass rod—tubular (or 'hollow glass' as it is often called) and solid. Of the two, solid glass is a good deal cheaper; but there can be no disputing the fact that a hollow glass rod is the superior weapon. For one thing it is lighter to handle, and possesses a pleasant steely action when casting or playing a fish. These admirable qualities make it ideal for shorecasting and spinning rods.

Indeed, there is so much extra pleasure to be obtained from shore fishing with a well designed and efficient rod that I would strongly advise you to buy the best one you can afford. On the other hand, the cheaper solid glass type of rod is quite satisfactory for deep-sea boat fishing; although, even in this field of operations, a hollow glass rod gives more enjoyable sport, and provides extra sensitivity to biting fish.

Just as sea rods vary considerably in their materials, workmanship and price, so do they also differ in length, thickness, taper, weight and various other details of design. The reason for this is that there are many different sea fishing methods, and each method requires a rod which possesses certain essential properties. Listed below are the main types of sea rod, with brief details of those factors which influence their design:

Pier Rods (i) For most kinds of pier fishing, lifting power is more important than ability to cast long distances. However, the rod must be reasonably flexible, so that it acts as a shock-absorber when a fighting fish makes a sudden run or dive. Length varies, but 8-9 ft. is popular. (ii) Light fishing is possible from some piers and jetties, using a rod similar to that described below under *Boat Rods* (ii).

Boat Rods (i) Bottom fishing from a boat requires a rod with sufficient lifting power, and this varies according to the strength of the local tides, species of fish, etc. For example, deep-sea fishing for large skate and conger requires a really powerful rod with considerable lifting power. Length varies, but about 7 ft. is popular. (ii) In the lighter forms of boat fishing, such as float fishing and driftlining, liveliness of the rod is the more important consideration. It should be flexible without being 'sloppy'; thus enabling the hook to be driven home from a distance, and large fish to be played firmly.

Shore Casting Rods (i) Casting ability, coupled with good pulling power and steely flexibility when playing a fish, are the most important things to look for when choosing this type of rod. An 11-12 ft. rod, casting about 4 oz. of lead, is recommended for *average* coastal conditions.

Float Fishing Rods. Most types of sea rod can be used for float fishing, but a light beach caster or a medium-length spinning rod will be found particularly suitable for most conditions. The rod should be lively, but stiff enough to pick up line quickly and drive the hook home when striking. The length varies according to local conditions, **but 9-10 ft. is popular for jetty fishing.**

Spinning Rods vary considerably in design, and the various types are discussed at length in Chapter 4.

From the foregoing facts it will be seen that the would-

Choosing the Right Tackle

be sea angler should have a fairly clear idea of the sort of fishing he intends to take up before visiting a tackle shop to buy his first rod.

If he wishes to concentrate on one particular branch of fishing, it will be a comparatively simple task to select a suitable rod by following the more detailed suggestions set out in later sections of this book. Quite understandably, however, most beginners seek a 'general purpose' rod—and, as we have already explained, no such thing exists. Nevertheless, it is often possible to use one type of rod for two or three different kinds of sea fishing. For example, a 9 or 10 ft. spinning rod could also be used for float fishing off a rocky vantage point, or even for light bottom fishing from a sheltered estuary beach.

Certainly it is a waste of money to buy a rod made of inferior materials. Young anglers—and their parents—would be well advised to bear this in mind before buying a cheap 'boy's rod'.

One perfectly satisfactory way to cut costs is to build your own rod from a fibre-glass 'blank'. A number of firms specialise in 'build-it-yourself' rod kits for the handyman-angler, and details of these are advertised regularly in the various fishing journals. The kits are usually supplied with full instructions, together with the rod rings, whipping thread, handle corks and reel fittings.

Rod Fittings

Rings should be of hard stainless steel, or some other metal that is impervious to the corrosive effects of salt water. On rods designed for heavy boat fishing the rings may be fitted with a 'Sintox' core to prevent the line cutting into the metal. Unlike the old-fashioned porcelain-lined rings, which cracked very easily, 'Sintox' rings are capable of standing up to really hard knocks and rough handling. For a heavy duty boat rod, the pulley type of end-ring is also useful, particularly when fishing with monel or stainless wire line to overcome the combined effects of strong tides and deep water.

The rings on a casting rod need to combine lightness

with strength—and this applies equally to a light spinning rod or a powerful surfcaster. I have a particular liking for the 'Abuflex' type of ring, made from a continuous length of stainless steel wire. The actual ring, through which the reel line passes, is made in the form of a spiral which is designed to flex with the rod so as not to inhibit the natural action of the fibre-glass blank. This type of rod ring is extremely hard and highly resistant to grooving—and, most important of all—it is free from welds which create a source of weakness in other types of ring.

One important point, sometimes overlooked by beginners, is that a casting rod used with a fixed-spool reel should be fitted with a large stand-off butt ring to control the line as it comes swirling and coiling off the reel spool. It should also have suitably graduated intermediate rings to 'funnel' the line from the large butt ring to the small end-ring.

Reel Fittings. Several methods are used for clipping the reel to the rod handle. The simplest device consists of two sliding rings which grip the saddle of the reel and hold it in position. Originally these rings were made of corrosion-proof metal, but in more recent years nylon rings have made their appearance. Because they are pliable—and apparently very slightly elastic—they grip the reel very tightly.

Free-sliding fittings of this type are mostly used on light spinning rods designed for use with a fixed-spool reel. Their main advantage is that they allow the reel position to be varied in order to obtain the correct balance and casting grip.

Rather more sophisticated is the sliding reel seat which locks into position upon tightening a knurled nut. This type, too, is designed primarily for fixed-spool fishing, and is mostly confined to spinning rods.

A stronger, fixed type of screw reel fitting is often used on beach and boat rods. In this design the reel saddle is clamped firmly into channelled grooves by means of a locking nut. This is very useful for heavy deep-sea fishing and shorecasting, where it is essential for the reel to remain rigid under considerable strains.

Choosing the Right Tackle

Ferrules. It is important that the rod ferrules fit closely enough to create plenty of suction. On the other hand they must not be over-tight because a very definite point of weakness occurs in a pair of ferrules which cannot be fitted snugly together.

The female ferrule should have a reinforcing band around its rim, and this will need to be fairly substantial in the case of deep-sea and beach-casting rods. Also, the ends of the ferrules covered by whippings should preferably consist of a series of metal tongues which will flex with the bending of the rod. These cannot be seen, of course, but it is often possible to feel their outline underneath the whippings.

Some hollow glass casting rods are not fitted with metal ferrules. Instead, the end of one rod section is fitted with a tapered spigot which fits into the hollow end of the adjoining section. This system has two great advantages—it makes for a lighter rod, and the absence of a rigid metal ferrule allows the rod to flex in an uninterrupted curve right through its length. This results in greater casting power.

REELS

A reel must fulfil several conditions if it is to be satisfactory for sea fishing. It must be the right size and weight to balance the rod, and its strength, line capacity and salt water resistance should be adequate for the kind of fishing it will be required to perform. On these points the beginner can expect guidance from the tackle dealer, but he must decide for himself the *type* of reel to buy.

Four main types of reel are used for sea angling—centre-pin, multiplying, fixed-spool and side-caster. Each has its own particular advantages and limitations.

Centre-Pin. This is the oldest type of fishing reel, and the simplest and most primitive form consists of a revolving spool fitted with two winding handles—each handle being positioned so that it balances the other.

Nowadays, however, the majority of centre-pins are fitted with a number of refinements. The most important of these, from the sea angler's point of view, is the optional check—a pawl and cogwheel device which prevents line being stripped off the reel by a running tide, although it will yield to the sudden snatch of a fish. When casting or retrieving, this check can be switched into the 'off' position, and the reel then revolves freely.

Rather less important is the adjustable drag. This, when very lightly applied, can help the novice to avoid overruns and tangles when casting. Also, when applied more strongly, it can help to slow down a large running fish.

Fig. 1. Centre Pin Reel.

Although the centre-pin reel still has its devotees on certain parts of the coast, it has been very largely superseded by modern multiplier and fixed-spool reels which are a good deal more efficient, both for distance casting and playing a big fish.

Multiplier Reels are so called because, when retrieving line, the spool is geared to revolve several times for every turn of the handle. Varying considerably in size and line capacity, they are mainly used by sea anglers for distance surfcasting, general boat fishing and big game angling. For all these types of sea fishing the multiplier is unquestionably the number one choice of most experts. The novice, however, is likely to encounter some problems when casting with a multiplier for the first time. To understand why this should be, one must first become acquainted with the basic mechanics of the reel.

Before casting with a multiplier the line spool is disengaged from the gears and winding handle by pressing a small release button or lever. This leaves the spool free to revolve very freely so that when this type of reel is used

Choosing the Right Tackle

with a suitable surf rod it is possible to make casts ranging between 100-150 yards under normal fishing conditions. Of course, a certain degree of skill has to be acquired before one can hope to achieve results like this, but the problems and difficulties are not so great as some beginners seem to imagine.

The secret of success lies in delicate line control. As the weighted terminal tackle streaks out to sea, drawing the fine nylon line after it, the angler must occasionally brake the rapidly whirling spool with feather-light touches of his thumb.

Too much thumb pressure inevitably results in a shortened cast. Too little pressure, on the other hand, allows the spool to revolve too fast, so that it throws off more line than the lead can carry away when it begins to slow down near the summit of its trajectory. This will almost certainly result in a frustrating and time-wasting tangle.

Another critical moment occurs when the weighted terminal tackle hits the water. This slows down the lead very quickly indeed, and the angler must immediately apply increased thumb pressure to his reel spool. This is easy enough when he can see the splash of the lead hitting the water, but it can create quite a problem when shore fishing in the dark. For this reason many beach fishermen prefer to use a large capacity fixed-spool reel for night casting.

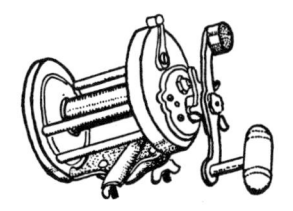

Fig. 2. Multiplier Reel.

Fixed-Spool Reels are very popular with sea anglers who specialise in the use of light tackle from shore, jetty or rocks. Although these reels were originally designed for freshwater fishing, many models are now available which have a high degree of resistance to salt water corrosion.

To the novice a fixed-spool reel may at first sight appear to be a rather complicated gadget. Yet it is really quite simple to use, and certainly makes casting very easy.

Fig. 3. A medium capacity fixed-spool reel with sea-proof specification.

From the accompanying illustration it will be seen that the spool containing the line lies at right angles to the rod butt. During the cast the line flows over the rim of the spool, the spool itself remaining stationary. Thus, with no moving or revolving parts, there is no inertia to overcome, and the possibility of a tangled line resulting from an overrun is eliminated.

During the retrieve a rotating pick-up arm snaps into position as soon as the handle is turned, and this guides the line back on to the spool. For sea fishing it is essential that this pick-up arm be strongly constructed, and vigorous in action. It should also be made of a very hard-wearing metal; otherwise the constant rubbing of the line will quickly wear a groove in it.

Nearly all fixed-spool reels also incorporate a slipping clutch of variable tension, which can be set to yield line automatically when the strain imposed by a fighting fish threatens to break the line. The tension at which the clutch is set naturally depends upon the breaking strain of the line. On some reels the setting screw is marked with a scale, so that the angler can easily re-set the clutch to a suitable tension after altering it while playing a fish, or for any other reason. This is quite a useful feature.

Line capacity is another important factor. It is most de-

Choosing the Right Tackle

sirable to choose a reel with interchangeable spools, so that lines of varying breaking strain can be used to suit different fishing methods. For most forms of salt water spinning, light float fishing, and medium-distance light ground fishing, a suitable reel would be one with a line capacity of about 200 yards at 12 lb. breaking strain, and 150 yards at 15 lb. breaking strain.

For long distance surf casting, however, it would be necessary to use one of the special large-capacity saltwater fixed-spools. These are efficient and popular with many anglers, particularly those who experience difficulty in casting with a multiplier reel.

Side-Casting Reels derive their name from the fact that while casting the drum is positioned sideways; or, in other words, at right angles to the rod butt. The line therefore spills over the edge of the drum in precisely the same way as it does with a fixed-spool reel. After the cast has been made, however, the position of the drum is altered, so that the reel becomes, in effect, a centrepin when recovering line or playing a fish. In this way one obtains the benefits of both types of reel.

One important point must be kept in mind, though, when choosing a reel of this type.

A side-casting reel sends the line out in a series of coils, which eventually become twists in the line. With the cheapest types of side-caster this line twist keeps building up every time the tackle is cast out, and eventually this may result in tangles unless the terminal tackle incorporates at least two swivels to remove the twists.

Side-casting reels are reputed to be popular with Australian surfcasters, but they have never really caught on with British shore fishermen.

LINES

Nowadays sea anglers use synthetic lines made of nylon, terylene, dacron, etc. Although all these materials are rotproof in the normal sense of the word, it is worth emphasising that they are weakened by prolonged exposure to the ultra violet rays contained in sunlight, and for this reason it is advisable to store your reels and spare line spools well away from sunny windows.

Synthetic lines are available in three forms—twisted, braided, and as a single strand commonly referred to as 'monofilament'.

Nylon Monofilament is very popular for many kinds of sea fishing, partly because its smooth surface allows it to flow freely off the reel when casting long distances, and partly because it is inconspicuous in the water.

However, it is worth mentioning that this type of line varies considerably in quality. The cheaper brands tend to be springy and intractable, and it is always worth paying a little extra in order to obtain a supple line that is pleasant to use.

A more serious drawback for certain types of fishing is the tendency of nylon monofilament to stretch under strain, making it difficult to strike (i.e. drive the hook home into a fish) when fishing at a distance.

Beginners must be very careful when tying knots in nylon monofilament, owing to the slippery and springy nature of this material. There is a correct knot for every purpose.

Braided Terylene is more expensive than nylon monofilament, but despite this it is popular with anglers who require a line which does not stretch under strain, and is inert and pleasant to handle. It is particularly useful for big-game and deep-sea fishing because the non-stretch qualities of this line enable the angler to drive home a big hook positively and firmly.

Twisted Nylon is very cheap, and this makes it useful as a rotproof 'backing line' for large capacity sea reels. On top of this backing line there is normally attached, by means of a blood-knot, a superior grade monofilament or braided line.

Wire Line. The very idea of deep-sea fishing with a wire line on their reel fills many boat anglers with horror. Yet in areas where the water is deep and tides run very hard, the use of a wire line makes it possible to fish at any time

Choosing the Right Tackle

over marks which are only fishable around slack water with ordinary nylon monofilament and braided terylene lines.

There are, in fact, three basic types of wire line suitable for use with rod and reel: monel metal, single strand stainless steel, and multi-strand stainless steel. Of these, the multi-strand type is the pleasantest to use—and the most expensive.

All types of wire line must be handled properly, and with reasonable care, if kinks and tangles are to be avoided. Monel metal wire is best used on a centre-pin reel with a large, narrow drum. The Pfleuger 'Pakron' reel, built on the 'cage and drum' principle, is excellent for this purpose, and as an added refinement it incorporates a one-way drag designed to operate only against the fish.

Stainless steel wire, both single and multi-strand, is best used with a *narrow* spool multiplier. The firm of Grice and Young produce a very good reel for this particular purpose.

Wire line also imposes extra wear on the rod rings. A roller-type tip ring is virtually a 'must' when using wire line. For intermediate rings, my own choice is the 'Sintox'-lined type.

As there is no elasticity at all in wire line, every bite and nibble at the bait is transmitted very distinctly to the rod-tip—even when fishing in a fast tide-rip in over thirty fathoms of water. This naturally makes it very easy for the angler to drive the hook into the fish, but by the same token the absence of line stretch also makes easy for a powerful fish to wrench itself off the hook again while it is being pumped to the surface.

To help overcome this problem it is standard practice to attach a 10-12 ft. nylon monofilament leader to the end of the wire line. The terminal trace is, in turn, attached to the end of the leader by means of a swivel-link. When legering, the sliding Clements boom and lead is threaded on the nylon leader, NOT on the wire line.

Two other points must be borne in mind when using wire line. If kinks are to be avoided, the line must be kept under a reasonable degree of tension all the time. There is normally no difficulty in achieving this, but a danger of

Complete Guide to Sea Fishing

kinking does occur on those occasions when another angler, fishing in the same boat, becomes entangled with your tackle, and reels up your trace along with his own. If this happens it is essential to reel in at the same time so as to avoid any slack forming in your line.

Finally, when using wire line, it is necessary to be very careful when trying to free tackle that has become snagged on the bottom. NEVER wrap the wire around your hand. This is dangerous practice even when using nylon line: with a wire line it could all too easily result in an amputated finger!

Always play for safety by putting two or three turns of line around the gaff handle, and using this to pull the tackle free.

To sum up, wire line can be invaluable for overcoming those occasional fast tidal conditions when deep-sea boat fishing, but for *average* fishing conditions it is much better to use a line made of braided terylene or dacron, or nylon monofilament.

TACKLE SUNDRIES

Apart from rod, reel and line, the sea angler will require a selection of hooks, traces, leads and swivels, together with a bait-box, a sharp knife for cutting up baits, and a

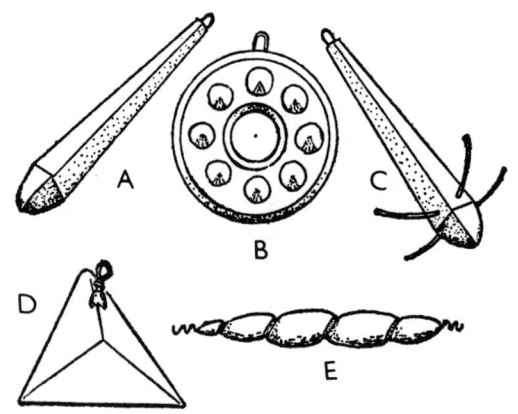

Fig. 4. Selection of sea leads. A—Torpedo, B—"Grip", C—"Anchor", D—"Capta", and E—Spiral.

Choosing the Right Tackle

tackle box fitted with a carrying strap. The tackle box should preferably be divided into a number of compartments, so that everything does not become hopelessly jumbled up.

The above list includes only the bare essentials. The wise angler will also carry a gaff or landing net (depending on the type of fishing), a pair of long-nosed pliers for removing hooks and making up wire traces, a fine carborundum slip for sharpening hooks, a torch for night fishing, and a rag for wiping bait-slimy hands.

The thickness of your hooks should be governed by the test curve, or pulling power, of the rod being used.

For instance, a heavy-gauge hook is essential when one is after large conger or skate with a powerful boat rod.

On the other hand, when using a light and lively rod—perhaps for driftlining or float fishing—it would be absurd to use a stout wire hook. Such a hook needs a strong, quick strike to drive it into the fish, and the flexible rod would lack the necessary power to do this.

A fine-wire hook, however, could be driven home quite easily, and there would be no risk of it being straightened out by a powerful fish because the flexibility of the light rod would act as a shock-absorber.

Needless to say, when choosing fine-wire hooks it is particularly important to select only those of top quality. Avoid hooks which are over-brittle, or which straighten out too easily. A good hook feels springy when you try to bend it between your fingers.

It is important that the size of hook should suit the type and size of bait being used. A common mistake—especially when baiting with fish strips—is to use a bait that is too big for the hook, so that it prevents the barb from fixing in the fish's mouth.

Round bend hooks are best when using worm baits, and if intended for flatfish they should be long in the shank. Also, the hooks should be in new condition—not roughened by rust. It is almost impossible to make a neat job of threading a ragworm on to a rusty hook.

The need to avoid 'weak links' when selecting tackle

Complete Guide to Sea Fishing

sundries cannot be stressed too strongly. Most sea anglers use brass swivels, because these are not greatly affected by salt water. Nevertheless, there is bound to be a gradual reduction in strength owing to wear and oxidisation, and

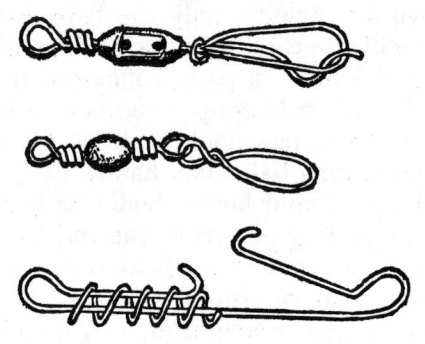

Fig. 5. Swivel links and clips.

an adequate safety margin should always be allowed for this.

Size for size, swivelled link-springs are probably somewhat stronger than swivel buckles when new. But the steel clip corrodes very quickly in salt water, and unless frequently checked it can become a dangerous source of weakness in one's tackle.

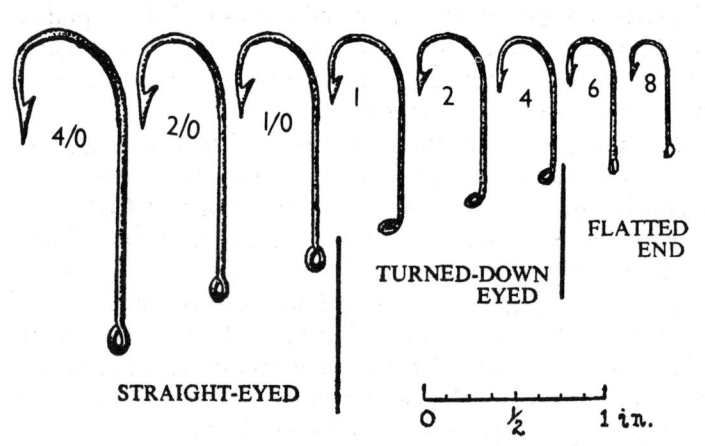

Fig. 6. Scale of sea hooks — actual size.

Choosing the Right Tackle

Much stronger than either of these, however, is the stainless steel spiral clip illustrated in Fig. 5. Although too conspicuous and cumbersome for light fishing, this type of clip is ideal for tope and conger traces.

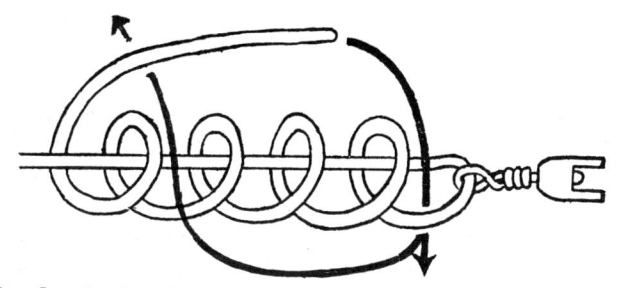

Half-Blood Clinch Knot for attaching line to any eyed item of tackle. (Knot strength 98%).

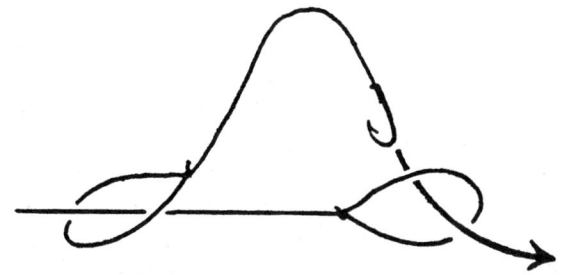

Method of joining Loop Knots.

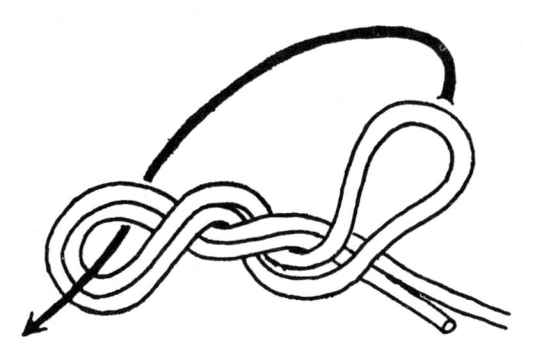

Loop Knot at end of the line or trace.

CHAPTER 2

Pier, Harbour Wall and Rock Fishing

THE novice sea angler, who has yet to master the art of casting long distances with rod and reel, will find that a pier or harbour wall provides the simplest means of getting his baited tackle out into reasonably deep water.

It is also a fact that such places often possess a special attraction for fish. Bass, pollack, coalfish, wrasse, mullet, pouting and various other species frequently swim close in to feed on the prawns and other small marine creatures which lead a furtive existence among the seaweedy piles and masonry. Conger, too, are likely to be lurking in the crevices between sea-eroded stonework, and there is no telling what size these big eels may run to. Many weighing 30 lb. or more are taken from harbour breakwaters, and even from estuary landing stages.

Fish hooked close in to a pier create a special problem for the angler, because there is always a risk that they will seek refuge amongst the piles. Certain species, such as pollack and wrasse, and sometimes bass, seem to do this deliberately, and it nearly always results in a broken line.

To prevent this sort of thing happening it is necessary for pier anglers to keep a fairly tight rein on fighting kinds of fish, and for this reason many use a firm (NOT rigid) rod with plenty of lifting power. A length of about 8 ft. is as much as most people can handle comfortably on the crowded type of pleasure pier, but a slightly longer rod may be used for jetty and harbour wall fishing.

Another reason for choosing a reasonably firm rod is that it is often necessary to reel hooked fish twenty feet or more from the sea to the deck of the pier. It will be appreciated, of course, that as soon as a fish is lifted out of the water it puts a much greater strain on rod and line, and this is the critical moment when so many big ones get away.

Pier, Harbour Wall and Rock Fishing

To overcome this difficulty the wise pier angler equips himself with a drop-net. This is simply a deep pouch-shaped net, with its open end laced to an iron hoop. Fitted with a long rope, it can be lowered over the side of the pier to retrieve fish of above-average weight. Some piers provide a drop-net for visiting anglers, but it is always more satisfactory to have one's own, ready for use at a moment's notice.

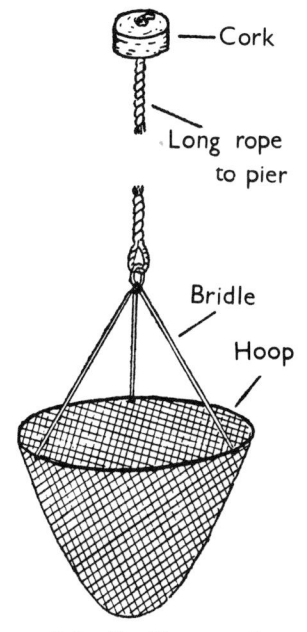

Fig. 7. Drop-net.

When making a drop-net it is a good idea to bind the iron hoop with strips of old tarpaulin or oilskin. This will prevent the netting from being weakened through coming into contact with the rusty iron.

When no drop-net is available it may be possible to play a sizable fish along the pier to a flight of steps, where it can be landed at water level. However, this will mean that other anglers fishing between you and the steps will first

Complete Guide to Sea Fishing

have to reel in their lines; so on a crowded pier these tactics can only be resorted to when a really exceptional fish has been hooked.

FISHING METHODS

The fishing methods used from a pier or harbour wall depend very largely upon local sea conditions and the species of fish found in that area. The following are the methods most commonly employed:

Float Fishing

Float tackle is largely used to catch those fish which swim between mid-water and the surface, such as bass, mackerel, scad and garfish. When the water is fairly shallow, however, float gear can also be adjusted to catch pollack, wrasse, bream and other species which normally swim quite near the sea-bed.

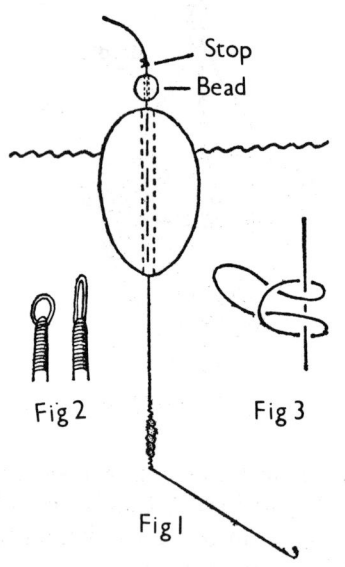

Fig. 8. Sliding Float Tackle.

There is a special fascination to be found in watching a float, and waiting for it to dip and suddenly disappear. All too often, though, the beginner's chances of experiencing

Pier, Harbour Wall and Rock Fishing

this thrill are spoilt by his using the wrong sort of float, or by setting up his tackle in the wrong way.

When float fishing at a depth greater than the length of one's rod, it is necessary to use a sliding float. (See Fig. 8).The reason for this, of course, is that a fixed float would jam against the end ring of the rod when reeling in, leaving a hooked fish dangling out of reach, or still swimming around in the sea. A sliding float, on the other hand, slips down the line when taken out of the water, and comes to rest just above the lead. This makes retrieving and casting quite easy.

There are various kinds of sliding floats to suit all sorts of conditions, but for medium fishing from a pier I use a cigar-shaped float made of balsa wood, which is threaded on the line by means of a hole running through the centre. On the other hand, when fishing from a harbour wall or estuary jetty, in calm water and at a fairly shallow depth, it is often preferable to use a small cork-bodied river float.

Some form of 'stop', of course, has to be put on the line to limit the upwards movement of a sliding float, and so control the fishing depth.

Various stops have been described in previous sea angling books, but nearly all of them are difficult to untie or re-position once they have been placed on the line. This trouble is aggravated after playing a heavy fish, owing to the fact that the knot or clove-hitch becomes tightened, and on being removed it leaves a kink in a light monofilament line.

The elastic band stop, illustrated in Fig. 8 (3), is free from all these faults. After it has been drawn tight the surplus elastic should be cut off.

Alternatively, if you do not happen to have an elastic band handy, you can snip a couple of inches of nylon monofilament off the end of your reel line, afterwards tying it tightly around the line with a reef knot, and cutting off the surplus.

This, too, makes an excellent stop, which can be slid up and down the line as required. It works best when made from monofilament of about 15-20 lb. breaking strain.

Both these stops are small enough to pass through the rod rings easily when casting. Indeed, you may even find that they are small enough to pass through the hole in the middle of the float—which would, of course, defeat their object. However, this problem can be overcome by threading a bead on the line between the float and the stop, as shown in Fig. 8.

In the case of a quill float the line will run through two wire eyes, and to prevent the stop passing through these it is only necessary to close the top eye slightly with a pair of pliers. (See Fig. 8).

Choosing the correct size of float is of prime importance. It should be only just large enough to support the leaded trace; and the lead should be only just heavy enough to take the bait down to the desired depth against the pull of the tide. An over-buoyant float presents too much resistance to a taking fish, and may arouse its suspicions so that it ejects the bait before the hook can be driven home.

For obvious reasons light float gear, weighted with only a few split shot, cannot be cast as far as a medium-sized float carrying possibly a small spiral lead.

Nevertheless it is sometimes necessary to cast light float tackle for a good distance, and in order to achieve this a small bubble float can be substituted for the customary quill float.

A bubble float is a hollow plastic sphere, fitted with two tiny plugs so that it can be filled, or partly filled, with water. The amount of water let into it controls its buoyancy. When almost filled, a small bubble float will just support a small bait and a few split shot; yet this light tackle casts well because the water in the float makes it quite heavy, and gives it plenty of momentum.

When float tackle is cast out any distance there will be a tendency for a nylon or terylene line to sink into the water, so that it hangs in a long sagging loop. A slack line like this makes it impossible to strike quickly when the float indicates a bite.

Pier, Harbour Wall and Rock Fishing

To overcome this problem it is possible to treat the line with a floatant. There are several brands on the market, but for a braided nylon line a cheap alternative is medicinal paraffin, obtainable from any chemist.

Yet another method of preventing line-sag is to reel in slowly between frequent casts. This is, in fact, a favourite method of West Country harbour wall and rock anglers, because keeping the bait on the move in this way also helps to stimulate pollack bites. A fixed-spool reel is very useful for this type of fishing.

So much for the basic principles of float fishing. But the real art of it lies in deciding upon the species you wish to catch, and then presenting a suitable bait on the right-sized hook, at the correct depth, and in the most likely place. However, there is no need to pursue this aspect of float fishing here, because the habits, haunts, fishing methods and baits for all the main species of British sea fish are dealt with fully in Chapter 9.

Driftline Fishing

Driftlining is a method of fishing above the bottom, using the buoyant effect of the tide instead of a float to keep the bait positioned at the desired depth. Although mainly a boat fishing method (see Chapter 7 for full details), driftlining can also be carried on from the down-tide side of a pier or jetty built on piles, and sometimes from the *end* of a stone pier jutting out into a tideway.

The tackle is simplicity itself, and the single hook can often be tied direct to the reel line. But when using baits which tend to twist in the flow of tide, it is advisable to insert a swivel in front of an anti-kink spiral lead.

The fishing depth is controlled by adjusting the amount of lead to balance the strength of the tide. As the tidal strength is bound to vary from hour to hour, a good selection of quick-change spiral leads should be carried. When the tidal flow is very slight, or when fishing for near-surface species, it may be unnecessary to use any lead at all.

Ground Fishing

Fish which feed on or very close to the sea-bed, such as conger, dogfish, skate and flatfish, are usually caught by placing the baited hook or hooks on the bottom. Listed below are the various types of ground fishing tackle favoured by pier and harbour wall anglers. When making up these traces in nylon monofilament, beginners should be careful to use the correct knots, illustrated elsewhere in this book.

The Paternoster. For general ground fishing there is much to be said in favour of a light and inconspicuous paternoster made up from nylon monofilament. (See Fig. 9). It can be cast out and left lying on the sea-bed; or, if the bottom is snaggy with rocks and weed, it can be suspended on a tight line—preferably on the down-tide side of the pier. In the latter case a position about 1 to 3 feet above the bottom usually gives good results.

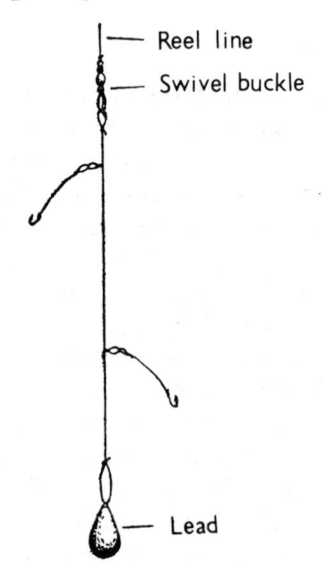

Fig. 9. Nylon Monofilament Paternoster.

Pier, Harbour Wall and Rock Fishing

The Paternoster-trot (Fig. 10) is a form of tackle that often produces good results on sandy or shelly ground where flatfish are common. It is also popular with codling anglers in some areas. It should be allowed to rest on the bottom, and is not recommended for tight-lining.

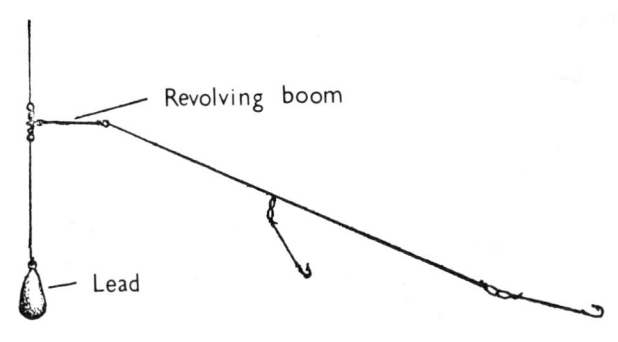

Fig. 10. Paternoster-trot

The Free-Running Leger (Fig. 11) is specially suitable for suspicious ground-feeding species, such as conger, which glide away with a bait before gorging it. With this form of leger tackle the fish feels no resistance from the lead when it pulls at the bait, because the reel line slides through the hole or eye in the lead.

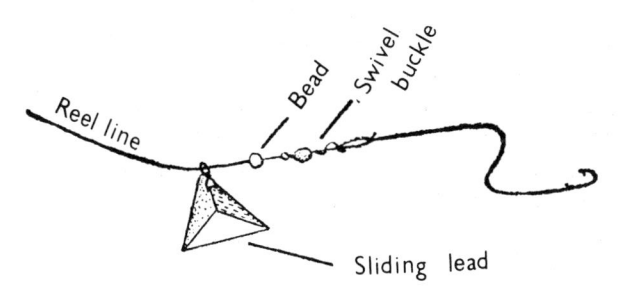

Fig. 11. Free-Running Leger.

The Wessex Leger (Fig. 12) is popular in a variety of forms with bass anglers on the Dorset coast and elsewhere. It combines the advantages of the paternoster with those of the free-running leger. Although originally devised for shore casting, it offers useful possibilities for the pier or harbour wall fisherman when the bottom is reasonably free of snags.

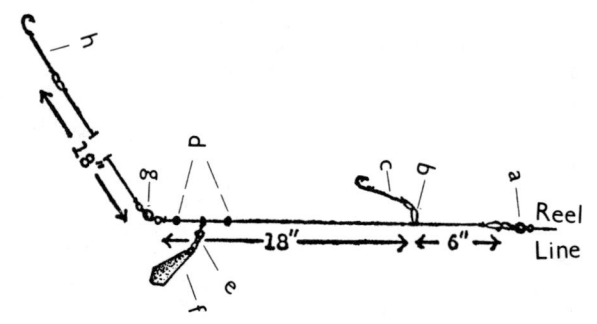

Fig. 12. Wessex Leger. A—Swivel clip, B—Paternoster Blood Loop, C—4" Snood, D—Sliding Beads, E—Sliding Clip, F—Lead, G—Swivel, H—6" Snood.

Sunken Float Tackle (Figs. 13 and 14). Using a float UNDER the water is a popular dodge with pier and harbour wall anglers in some districts. The object behind the idea is to lift a light monofilament paternoster or a single flowing trace a foot or two above the sea-bed, thereby making the baits more attractive to species which normally feed near, but not right on, the bottom.

Of course, when fishing close in beside the pier or jetty, the tackle could be suspended just above the sea-bed on a tight line. However, there are many occasions when this is inconvenient. There may be obstructions on the sea-bed close in, or wrasse may be waiting to carry the baited hook into crevices in the masonry of the jetty.

Under these circumstances the angler will have to cast some distance out, but a sunken float still enables him to keep his tackle off the sea-bed as though he were tight-lining.

Pier, Harbour Wall and Rock Fishing

If reeled in briskly when retrieving, this tackle will also swim upwards over any intervening rocks or other obstructions.

Fig. 14, it will be noted, shows a form of leger-cum-paternoster which enables bottom fishing for conger, skate, dogfish or flatfish to be combined with near-bottom fish-

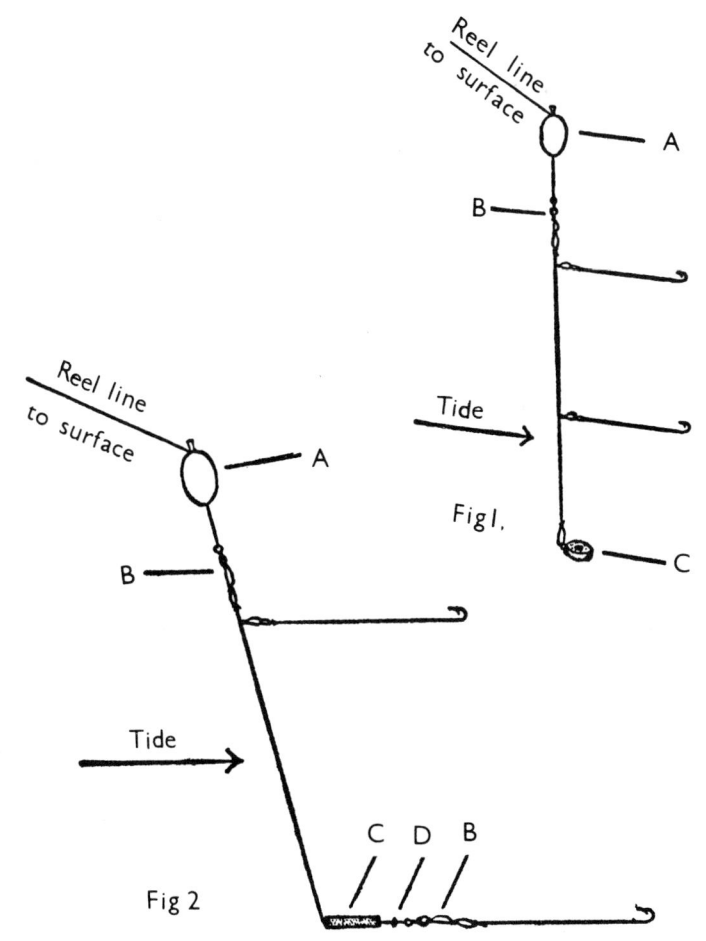

Figs. 13 and 14. Sunken Float Tackles. A—Float, B—Swivel Clip, C—Lead, D—Lead Shot.

ing. My own experience, however, is that it cannot be cast out so far as the terminal gear shown in Fig. 13; nor can it be retrieved as easily over intervening snaggy ground.

Spinning

Spinning is becoming increasingly popular with sea anglers when fishing from harbour walls, suitable rocks, estuary revetments and landing stages, etc. It is a very specialised form of fishing, and the subject is dealt with fully in Chapter 4.

ROCK FISHING

Most of what has already been written about pier and harbour wall fishing applies equally well to rock fishing. It should be realised, though, that the rock angler often has to cope with special problems and difficulties, and his tackle may have to be modified accordingly. For instance, rocks often have sloping sides below water level, and are usually surrounded by trailing fronds of weed. To steer fish clear of these snags may require a fairly long rod of about 10-11 ft. This applies in particular to areas where wrasse and pollack are found, as these two species will deliberately try to head for the nearest cover when they feel the hook.

On some coasts rock fishing is a pretty rugged pastime, so the angler should not burden himself unnecessarily with tackle. However, a long-handled landing net or gaff should always be carried.

For the adventurous and sure-footed, night fishing from the rocks often yields excellent results, especially in places where it is possible to fish on the bottom for conger. Don't forget to take a strong sack for the catch!

The safest form of illumination for this kind of fishing is an electric lamp worn on the forehead by means of an elastic band. This leaves both hands free, and the beam automatically follows the direction one is looking.

Finally, a word of warning. The rock angler must always be on his guard against becoming cut off by a rising tide, or falling on wet and slippery rocks. Rocks covered with green silk weed are particularly treacherous underfoot.

CHAPTER 3

Beach Fishing

THE angler who wishes to try his hand at beach fishing must, of course, possess the necessary skill and tackle to get his baited hooks out to where the fish are feeding. For example, on a flat sandy shore it may be necessary to cast out 100 yards or more; whereas from a steeply shelving bank of shingle, with deep water close inshore, a cast of only 25 yards, or even less, may be adequate.

The novice shore angler would therefore be well advised to begin by visiting a steeply shelving beach, where a high standard of casting is not essential.

Because of the widely differing conditions encountered around our coasts it is impossible to lay down any hard and fast rules concerning the choice of rod and reel, but the general trend nowadays is to fish as light as is reasonably possible, using a sensibly balanced outfit that will deal efficiently not only with the general run of shore fish, but also with a fairly wide range of beach conditions.

Not even the most versatile rod will cope satisfactorily with *all* types of shore fishing, however, and the subject is best considered under two headings: surf fishing, and fishing from sheltered beaches.

Surf Fishing

The majority of anglers who fish from exposed beaches favour a rod about 11½ ft. long, designed to cast a weight in the region of 4 oz. In some areas, however, where the surf is very heavy, or the tides are exceptionally strong, it may be necessary to use 6 oz. or more of lead; in which case, of course, a more powerful rod will be required to cast the additional weight.

A beach rod should develop a good brisk action when

used with the correct casting weight. A lead that it too light for the rod will not fully develop this action, and in consequence it will be impossible to achieve the maximum casting distance.

A more common fault, however—and a much more serious one—is to use a lead that is too heavy for the rod. This, too, results in loss of power when casting, and the rod is likely to be strained in the process.

Some enlightened rod manufacturers mark their products with a recommended casting weight, but in the absence of this information you will have to discover it for yourself by trial and error. However, a close approximation may be arrived at in the first instance by noting the *minimum* pull, in pounds, needed to flex the rod through an arc of about 60 degrees. This can be done by running a short length of line from the end-ring of the rod to a spring balance hooked to the floor. When doing this, the rod should be held by the butt in the normal way.

The resulting balance reading, in pounds, is known as the test curve loading, and this gives an indication, in *ounces*, of the ideal casting weight to use with that particular rod. For example, a rod which has a 4 lb. test curve may be used with a 4 oz. lead.

It must be stressed, however, that this test should only be used on proper casting rods, built of really flexible materials such as split cane and fibre-glass.

Although it should possess a lively action, a beach rod must also be firm enough to drive the hook home into a fish from a considerable distance. The rod should also be reasonably light, so that it can be held for long periods without fatigue.

However, the rod and reel must also be properly matched if they are to *feel* light and comfortable in use. The tackle dealer, if he knows his job, will be able to advise the beginner on this point.

The most popular types of reel for beachcasting are the multiplier and the fixed-spool. In Chapter 1 we have already discussed the comparative merits and disadvantages of these two reels, and the only other point I wish to

Beach Fishing

make at this stage is that, *once mastered*, a multiplier is the more efficient reel for distance casting with leads weighing upwards of 3 ounces.

When casting a similar amount of lead with a fixed-spool reel, there is a tendency for the line to cut into one's forefinger immediately before the moment of release. This can be particularly painful when winter fishing with hands numbed with cold.

A fixed-spool reel should always be loaded with nylon monofilament, and the same type of line can also be used with a surfcasting multiplier—provided you choose a brand that is soft and supple.

The big advantage of nylon monofilament is that it has a smooth surface, and therefore offers less resistance to wind, waves and tide than a braided line of equal strength. This, in turn, results in longer casts and (as a general rule) greater fishing efficiency.

Nevertheless, braided dacron and terylene can be used with a multiplier, and because of its non-stretch properties some anglers prefer this type of line when casting short distances in rocky areas for conger.

Line strength? On an exposed coast this may vary from about 18 lb. to 35 lb. breaking strain—and an even stronger line is sometimes necessary under exceptional circumstances. The strength of the line depends mainly upon the nature of the sea-bed, the amount of lead used, the inertia resistance of the reel when casting, and the test curve of the rod.

Contrary to popular belief, the size of the fish likely to be caught is not a very important consideration when deciding the strength of line to be used—assuming, of course, that the angler can play the fish with average skill.

It might be appropriate at this stage to offer some guidance to the beginner on casting with a multiplier reel. There are various individual and local styles of casting, but in all cases the essentials for success are identical.

The first essential is to understand what happens to the weighted tackle during the cast. Upon leaving the rod it travels swiftly upwards and outwards in an arc, slowing down gradually as it nears the upper limits of its trajectory, and then gaining speed once more as it begins to fall towards the water. As it enters the sea, the tackle is checked again, but much more abruptly, by the resistance of the water.

On the two occasions when the tackle slows down there is a risk that the freely spinning reel will throw out line more quickly than the lead can carry it away. Should this happen the result will be a particularly horrible sort of tangle, known to fishermen as a 'bird's-nest'.

To counteract this tendency, therefore, the reel drum must be controlled throughout the cast by the merest feather-light touch of a finger on the rim. Finally, the instant before the terminal tackle enters the sea, the reel must be checked almost completely.

The novice should not strive to cast long distances to begin with, but should try instead to acquire a smooth and powerful swing of the arms and shoulders. Distance will come automatically when the necessary style has been acquired.

For those who wish to cast long distances without any risk of bird's-nests, there are many excellent makes of medium and large capacity fixed-spool reels. Most experts prefer the fish-playing qualities of the multiplier reel, but there's no denying that a fixed-spool makes casting much easier—especially in the dark.

So much for rods, reels and lines. Now let us take a look at the terminal tackle.

Fishing from exposed beaches is mostly carried on by casting out some form of nylon monofilament leger or paternoster, and allowing it to lie on the bottom. (See Figs. 9 and 12). Provided that the sea-bed is not snaggy, it is often a good thing to retrieve the tackle very slowly with a turn or two of the reel every thirty seconds or so. Not only will this prevent the trace from becoming buried or jumbled up by the surge and backwash of the surf, but the occasional movement helps to arouse the interest of fish.

On the other hand, if the sea-bed is at all snaggy it is

Beach Fishing

usually advisable to let the tackle lie undisturbed after it has been cast out. Of course it will be necessary to reel in occasionally to make sure that the bait has not been stripped from the hook by crabs, but the frequency of these inspections can be reduced by using firm baits, such as squid.

If the sea-bed is very snaggy it may be impossible to use ground-tackle at all. But if the bottom is merely 'scrubby', with numerous small rocks scattered over sand or grit, it is sometimes possible to fish on the bottom by using a 6 in. length of bicycle tyre inner tube packed with wet sand in place of the customary lead weight. This 'sandbag sinker', as it is commonly called, will rise up through the water when retrieved swiftly, carrying the tackle safely over intervening rocks and weed. It can only be used in reasonably calm conditions, however, as it does not hold bottom where there are breaking waves or strong tides.

Naturally this type of sinker needs a few yards of reasonably snag-free sea-bed in order to 'take-off', and the

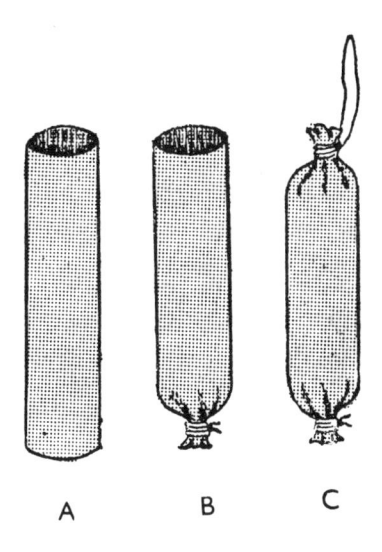

Fig. 15. Drawing showing how to make a sandbag sinker.

best way to locate a suitable spot is to carry out a preliminary survey of the beach at low tide. Alternatively, when the water is clear, it is often possible to pinpoint the position of submerged inshore rocks by obtaining a gull's-eye view from a cliff-top. The rocky areas will be clearly discernible as dark patches against the lighter expanses of sandy ground.

Beginners may wonder why anyone should risk losing tackle by casting out close to rocks, when there are so many other beaches unencumbered with snags.

The reason is that many species of fish are attracted to rocky areas. Some, like conger, actually live among the rocks; others merely visit them in passing, as it were, in search of prawns, shore crabs, and other small food creatures.

Indeed, any shoreline that is rich in small marine life is usually a good place to fish. On flat sandy shores one should concentrate on those places where the lugworm casts, or the razorfish holes, are thickest. Weed beds, too, are happy hunting grounds for fish, and tackle cast out on to clean ground near the fringe of a weed patch will often produce results.

In calm weather the lugworms, razorfish and other burrowing creatures remain in more or less safe concealment from predatory fish. But when there is a good run of surf many of these food organisms get scooped out of the sand by the back-scour, and it is then that bass come close inshore to feed on them. On a shore with an average slope the greatest concentration of food (and therefore of fish) is often to be found where the retreating water of the back-scour collides violently with the advancing surge of the next wave—and it is just a few yards beyond this area that the angler should endeavour to place his baits. For obvious reasons these baits should, if possible, correspond with the natural food of the bass at that particular time and place.

On a gently shelving stretch of sand, however, the collision between advancing and retreating waves is not nearly so marked, and a more likely area for placing the

Beach Fishing

bait is just beyond the white water. Incidentally, it should be noted that a *very* heavy surf does not as a rule produce good fishing. The best catches are usually made *after* a fresh onshore blow, when the swell waves are surging powerfully, but not violently, up the beach.

Fishing in Sheltered Water

On shores protected from prevailing winds and strong tides it is often possible to use ground tackle carrying only 1½ ounces or so of lead. This opens up possibilities of excellent sport, using a light and lively rod. Local conditions, of course, are bound to dictate one's choice of tackle to a certain extent; but a typical outfit for this type of fishing would consist of a 9 or 10 ft. bass spinning rod, and a medium-capacity fixed-spool reel loaded with a line of 10-15 lb. breaking strain.

The terminal tackle usually consists of a two-hook nylon monofilament paternoster, or a leger carrying either one or two hooks. The Wessex Leger (see Fig. 12) is particularly useful, as it casts quite well, and baits presented on it appeal to a wide variety of fish.

Nowadays light shore fishing of this nature is carried on to a considerable extent in estuaries, large artificial harbours and sheltered bays. Even on exposed coasts, however, it is sometimes possible to find sheltered conditions —in 'corners' protected by headlands, for instance; or in sandy gullies flanked by out-jutting rock ledges or scaurs.

From sheltered beaches which have a sufficient depth of water close inshore it is also possible to use float fishing and spinning methods for bass, mackerel and sometimes (near rocks) pollack. Likely spots for this are steep-shelving spits of sand or shingle; open shingle beaches when the wind is blowing offshore; and beaches bordering tide-scoured bottlenecks in estuaries. Flounders are also taken from suitable estuary shores by spinning with a baited-spoon. (See Chapter 9).

Playing the Fish

Playing a fish is both an art and a science. It consists of

manipulating the rod and reel in such a way that a large and powerful fish—perhaps many times 'stronger' than the line—is controlled, subdued, and eventually brought safely to the gaff or landing net.

When playing a fish, the angler should bear in mind the following points:

i. A flexible rod will act as a shock absorber whenever the fish makes a sudden rush or plunge, BUT ONLY when it is held well up (or sideways) against the pull exerted by the fish. The rod should therefore never be pointed at the fish.

ii. The rod, when properly held, can only exert a strain on the line equal to its test curve loading. So when using a properly balanced outfit there is no risk of the line breaking before the rod is fully bent to rather less than a quarter circle. It is assumed, of course, that the rod in question is really flexible, and capable (as a good split cane or fibreglass casting rod should be) of bending to this shape without risk of damage.

iii. When necessary the strain on the rod and line may be kept within the bounds of safety by allowing the fish to strip line from the reel. At the same time, however, sufficient pressure should be retained on the reel to keep the rod well and truly bent—either by manual pressure against the rim of the reel, or by applying the adjustable drag.

iv. The angler should grab every opportunity to recover line as soon as the fish begins to show signs of tiring. If it turns and begins to head back towards the shore, it is essential to reel in as fast as possible to avoid slack line, and if necessary the line should be kept taut by beating a hasty retreat up the beach, or along the water's edge. A slack line can quickly become tangled around the reel drum, and it may also allow the fish to rid itself of the hook.

Landing the Fish

Normally the beach angler will use a gaff, rather than a landing net, to land his large fish. This should be strong

Beach Fishing

and needle-sharp, and the handle should be long enough to provide a decent reach without being cumbersome to use. Conger eels delight in unscrewing the 'screw-in' type of gaff head, so this kind should only be used if fitted with a really secure locking device.

If a heavy sea is running, play the fish out while it is still some distance beyond the wave-breaks, and then reel

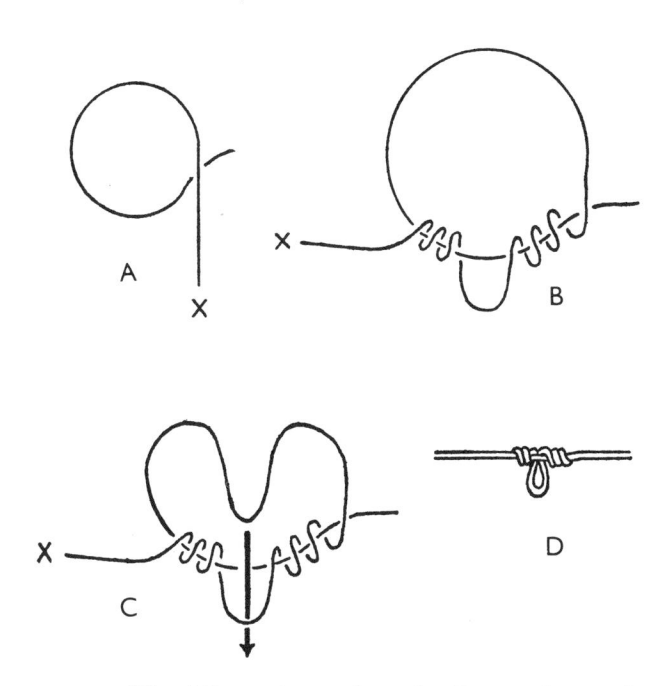

Paternoster Blood Loop for making hook-attachment loops in the middle of a nylon monofilament paternoster or similar trace. (Knot strength 80%).

Method of tying: A—Make a large circle of line where you wish to tie the loop. B—Twist end X around the circle three times, then leave a gap by inserting a finger between X and the circle of line—after which twist X around the circle another three times. C—Pull the top part of the circle through the gap in the twists. D—Pull knot tight, and a loop will be formed as shown.

it in so that it is helped by the surge of an incoming wave. When it lies stranded in the shallows, hold it against the drag of the back-scour, *keeping the rod well up,* and then hurry down and grab it, or gaff it, before the next wave comes in.

Never try to reel in a large fish against the out-going rush of the back-scour, or you will almost certainly lose it.

If the back-scour is very fierce, and it is obvious that one wave will not be sufficient to bring the fish within gaffing distance, the angler's best plan is to move further along the shore, keeping to the water's edge, until he is in a position to bring the fish in at an angle of about 45 degrees to the set of the waves. In this way the line is not subjected to a dangerous strain as soon as the back-scour catches the fish, because the fish is free to swing outwards on the angled line.

These tactics can be repeated as often as necessary—reeling in and edging along the shoreline with each incoming wave; and allowing the fish to swing out the back-scour on a tight line. On each occasion it should be possible to recover several yards of line, and before long, all going well, the fish will be within reach of the gaff.

CHAPTER 4

Spinning

SPINNING consists of casting out a natural or artificial bait, and then retrieving it through the water at a depth and speed likely to interest such predatory fish as bass, pollack, mackerel and coalfish. It can be a very sporting and rewarding method of fishing from rocks, jetty or steep-shelving beach, and every year it claims the attention of more and more sea anglers.

Because the spinning bait and trace must be light enough to 'swim' through the water, it is possible to use only a small amount of lead as an aid to casting. Lots of artificial baits have, in fact, all the necessary casting weight built into them, and no lead need be added to the trace. These are the easiest sort to use, because they are much less likely to double back and become tangled with the trace when casting.

Rods and Reels

There are two basic types of spinning outfit. The first—and by far the most popular with British sea anglers—is a light rod designed for use with a small to medium capacity fixed-spool reel. The length of the rod is usually about 7 to 7½ ft. for single-handed casting; or 9 to 10 ft. for two-handed casting.

The alternative choice is a 'baitcasting' rod designed primarily for use with a small levelwind multiplier. However, this sort of rod can also be used with one of the modern closed-face baitcasting reels, such as the well-known 'Abumatic'. Baitcasting rods are usually equipped with a cranked handle to make reel control easier.

My own preference lies with the fixed-spool outfit, mainly because it is capable of casting very light lures (down to

Complete Guide to Sea Fishing

only ¼ oz.) for comparatively long distances. Of course, a baitcasting multiplier also has its merits, but it only becomes an efficient weapon when casting fairly heavy lures weighing upwards of ⅞ oz. There will be many occasions in saltwater spinning when you will need to flick out a much lighter lure than this.

When spinning from harbour walls, or steep-sided and weed-free rocks, many anglers use a single-handed spinning rod and medium capacity fixed-spool reel loaded with 8-10 lb. b.s. nylon monofilament. This type of outfit is quite capable of beating a double-figure bass, and it is the ideal choice when spinning from a drifting dinghy where casting space is limited. For the same reason, a single-handed rod is also handy when shore spinning in places where you are hemmed in by tall boulders or a steep cliff face.

Alternatively, on coasts where the rocks are not so steep-to, or where fish have to be steered around clumps of seaweed, a longer two-handed rod will be found more suitable. With this type of outfit I would recommend using 10-12 lb. b.s. line.

Some sea anglers indulge in a rather crude form of spinning with their ordinary beachcasting or pier fishing outfits. In summer, when a shoal of mackerel ventures within casting range, these anglers hurriedly tackle up with a trace carrying three mackerel feathers and a 4 oz. lead. This is repeatedly cast out and retrieved through the shoal —often with considerable success. The secret is to keep the lead off the bottom while retrieving the feathers with an energetic pumping action of the rod. During this process, incidentally, the rod should be held horizontally, and more or less sideways to the sea.

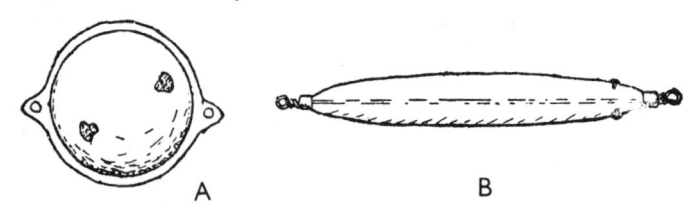

Fig. 16. Two types of bubble float.

Spinning

However, don't get the impression that I am recommending this makeshift spinning method. It is better than nothing... but the best sport, and the greatest pleasure, comes only by using the right tackle, properly balanced.

Lines and Traces

In any sort of fishing it is important to load one's reel with the correct type and weight of line—but especially is this true when spinning.

Nylon monofilament is the almost universal choice nowadays, not only of those who use a fixed-spool reel, but also for use on small levelwind multipliers and closed-face spincasters. It is essential, however, to choose a good quality line that is soft and supple, so that it flows smoothly off the reel spool. Cheap, inferior brands of nylon, on the other hand, are almost invariably springy and intractible, and this is a frequent cause of line tangles when spinning with a baitcasting multiplier.

Whatever type of reel is used, the weight of the line is all-important. Light baits require a light line ... as light as can be used with safety.

Other factors being equal, even a small reduction in the weight of the line—say from 12 lb. to 10 lb. breaking strain—can make a considerable difference to the distance one is able to cast.

When using a braided line it is, of course, advisable to have an inconspicuous trace between the line and the bait, and this may be of nylon monofilament. The fish taken by spinning in salt water—mackerel, bass, pollack and coalfish—are unlikely to damage monofilament with their teeth, although needless to say it is always wise to check the trace after landing a large specimen.

The length of the trace will vary with the length of the rod, and as opinions tend to differ on this subject it would be unwise to lay down any hard and fast rules. Most beginners, however, will find a 2 ft. trace about the easiest length to manage with a 7 ft. rod, and a 2-3 ft. trace with a two-handed 10 ft. rod.

Complete Guide to Sea Fishing

The majority of anglers fit a swivel-link at the end of a spinning trace to facilitate the attachment and removal of lures. It must be pointed out, however, that the attachment spring will soon corrode after use in salt water, and should be tested carefully at the start of every fishing session. It is, in fact, a wise plan to rinse it after use under a freshwater tap, together with the lure.

When spinning with a fixed-spool reel that is already loaded with monofilament, there is no particular need to use a trace unless it is considered necessary to prevent the line becoming twisted by fitting a swivel and anti-kink lead or vane a short distance from the lure.

As a rule the use of an anti-kink device is necessary only when using baits which actually revolve in the water; although beginners should note that many baits revolve even though they are not fitted with spinning 'wings' or 'propellors'. A rubber eel, for instance, spins vigorously when retrieved; and so, quite often, does an ordinary fish-strip bait.

There is no doubt that a ball-bearing swivel is the most efficient type for removing line twist. These are rather expensive, however, and a neat and economical alternative is the diamond-eyed swivel.

Like most other kinds of swivel, this type is not sufficiently free-running to remove twist by itself, and as al-

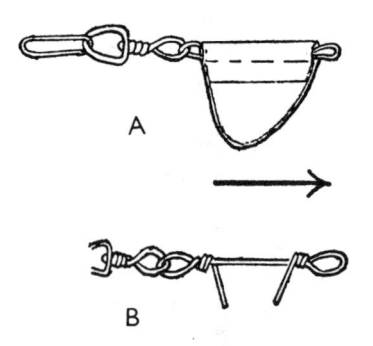

Fig. 17. How to make an Anti-Kink Lead. Sheet lead is folded over brass wire bent as in Fig. B.

Spinning

ready mentioned it will have to be used with an anti-kink vane or lead. When choosing an anti-kink lead, it is important to select a streamlined pattern which, when drawn through the water, does not create an air bubble or water disturbance, or become snagged on seaweed. Fig. 17 shows a suitable home-made type.

There is another type of anti-kink lead which can be fitted to the attachment eye of a spoon or other suitable

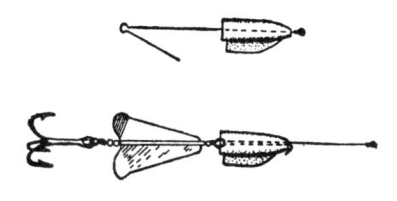

Fig. 18. Anti-kink head-lead.

lure. (See Fig. 18). This makes for easy casting, and there is practically no risk of the lure swinging back and fouling the trace. On the other hand, before using this type of lead it is necessary to make sure that it does not spoil the action of the lure.

Natural and Artificial Baits

When it comes to selecting a natural bait for spinning, most sea anglers will probably decide to try a small freshly-killed fish mounted on a spinning flight. Sprats, smelts, and tiny finger-length mackerel, pollack and whiting are all suitable, but a sandeel is perhaps best of all. The last-named bait should preferably be presented on a light home-made flight that allows some movement in the long flexible body.

When small whole fish are not available, it is possible to use a strip of mackerel or squid—possibly mounted behind a small spoon or spinner. Mackerel strips are best cut diagonally from the side of a freshly-caught fish, the length varying between 1½-3 inches according to whether or not the fish are 'biting short'.

On occasions I have had good catches of bass and pollack when spinning with strips of squid. These should be cut about three inches long, with a slightly curved shape and tapered tail, and mounted on the tandem-hook arrangement shown in Fig 36.

Artificial spinning baits possess a strange fascination for many sea anglers, and it is not an easy task to differentiate between those which are likely to catch fish, and those which are designed primarily to catch the angler who has some money in his pocket.

As a rough guide, however, most successful artificials simulate (no matter how crudely) the flickering or water vibrations caused by small fish when swimming. In other words, the points which really count are the lure's action in the water, and its ability to stimulate a predator's hunting instincts.

In the case of a revolving lure, a detailed biological similarity to the real thing is usually of little importance, but it does help if the lure *feels* natural when tentatively mouthed by a fish.

Some artificial baits are even designed to emit an interesting fishy *smell,* like the very attractive plastic sandeel perfected by Alex Ingram, of Mevagissey. The hollow plastic body of this lure can be loosely filled with cotton wool, and injected with an occasional squirt of pilchard oil from an oil can.

A tiny self-weighted chromed metal pirk is a useful lure for mackerel, especially when spinning off a beach of steeply-shelving shingle. So is a small self-weighted spoon with a twirling action, like the ABU 'Droppen' and 'Reflex' patterns. Silver, silver and red, and silver and blue are the best colours to use.

For bass you will probably decide to use something larger, although big bass of 10 lb. or more have been taken on tiny revolving spoons. Usually, though, an elongated wobbling spoon stands the best chance of arousing the interest of this species.

Spinning

I have also had good results with pollack and bass when using a 1-inch 'Vibro' spoon that had been modified by replacing the treble hook with a Pennell trace baited with ragworm.

Plugs and wagtails are two other useful kinds of lure for pollack and bass. Specially suitable for decent-sized pollack is the Swedish type of plug which has an adjustable lip, enabling the lure to be fished either deep, shallow or

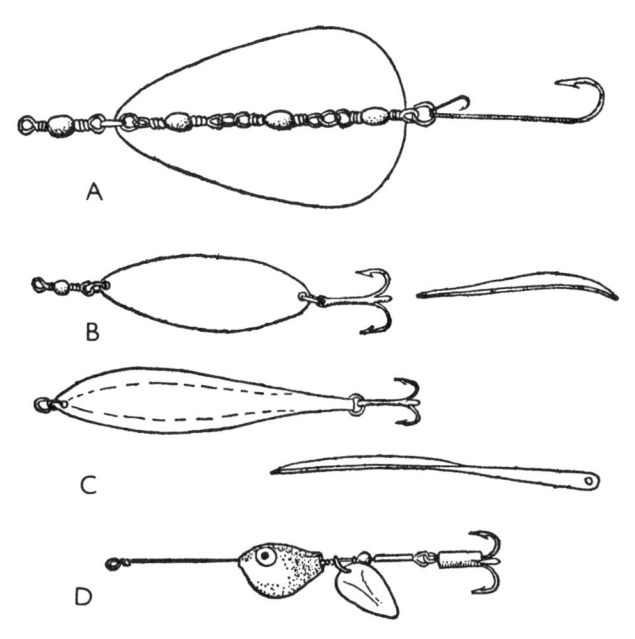

Fig. 19. A—Flounder spoon, B—Wobbling spoon, C—"Lurette", D—Voblex (last three useful for bass, mackerel and pollack).

in mid-water. Wagtails, on the other hand, are recommended mainly for bass, and my own preference lies with the type fitted with a single treble near the tail.

A buoyant plug is particularly suitable for rock fishing, because it can be made to rise over snags and patches of weed. Once the plug has been sent down to the required depth, it is reeled in slowly and erratically, so that in turn it flutters and dives, then drifts and rises to the surface. Used thus, in the early morning or evening, it can be very deadly for pollack. Some useful colours for salt water plugs are—blue back and silver belly; yellow back and sides, fluorescent orange hood and silver belly; and fluorescent red hood and white body. The fluorescent markings seem to stir pollack into action in the half-light of dawn and dusk.

Some Spinning Problems

Spinning in salt water has its own special problems. High tide, for instance, often requires different tackle and tactics to half-tide; whilst at low tide spinning may be impossible in some areas. Similar differences divide beach spinning from harbour wall and rock spinning.

If the coastline faces west, the prevailing onshore winds are likely to be a bugbear. The waves or swells may make rock stances inaccessible, and the wind itself makes casting difficult.

Under these conditions I plump for a lure with 'built in' weight, using the minimum of additional lead above the trace. Not only can this type of lure be cast a reasonable distance into an onshore breeze, there is also much less risk of it doubling back on the line while in flight and becoming hitched up.

However, it is sometimes argued that a lure which possesses built in weight is unlikely to feel natural to a fish. This may be true of lures which are particularly heavy in relation to their size, but most well designed loaded lures are by no means heavy once they are immersed in water.

Nevertheless there are circumstances under which a light lure, used with a lead above the trace, will definitely yield better results. For example, imagine two anglers spinning from a fairly high harbour wall.

Angler A uses a lure with the weight built in; while B uses a light lure with the lead positioned several feet ahead. (See Fig. 20).

When being retrieved, A's lure adopts the same angle as the reel line, and for obvious reasons this angle becomes

Spinning

steeper as the line is reeled in. This makes the lure appear unnatural to predatory fish, especially the larger and more experienced ones.

Now consider B's tackle. The line still rises at a gradually steepening angle between the lead and the rod-tip, but the trace between the lead and the lure remains almost horizontal. Thus the action and general appearance of the lure is more natural.

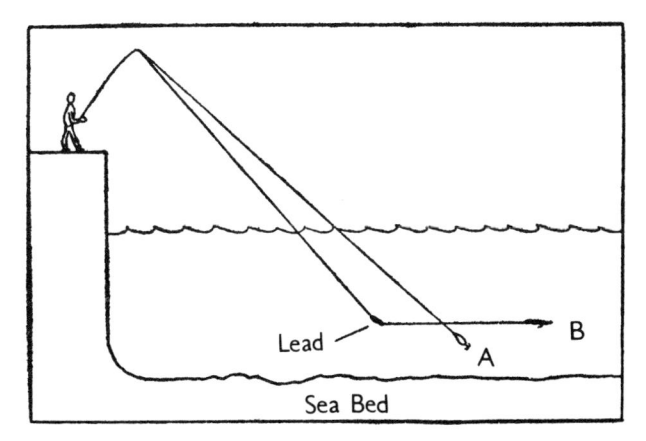

Fig. 20. Advantage of a light lure when spinning from a position well above the level of the water.

The closer one fishes to the surface of the water, the less need there is to take this aspect of spinning into account, although a certain amount also depends upon the length of one's rod and the depth of the lure beneath the surface.

Some very pleasant and productive spinning can be obtained from a steeply shelving beach, either on an open stretch of coast, or from a spit of sand or shingle jutting out into an estuary channel. Here one is fishing right at the water's edge, and there is little to choose between the retrieve angle adopted by the two types of lure.

Even when using a long rod, the gentle climb of the loaded lure towards the surface appears natural enough, because a real fish would have to do the same when it found the sea-bed sloping upwards towards the shore.

From the foregoing facts it will be appreciated that before setting up one's spinning tackle it is necessary to study local conditions, and to weigh up the advantages and disadvantages of the different types of lure.

CHAPTER 5

Sea Fishing with Freshwater Tackle

INLAND anglers often wonder whether it would be possible to use their freshwater rods and reels for sea fishing while holidaying at the coast.

This sort of problem cannot be answered with a brief 'yes' or 'no', because so many variable factors are involved, such as the shore conditions at the place in question, the strength of the tides and surf, the sea fishing methods to be used, and the species of fish likely to be encountered.

The risk of damage to reels, rod fittings and landing net due to salt water corrosion must also be considered. This risk can be reduced considerably, however, if everything is rinsed thoroughly under a freshwater tap after each fishing session.

Fortunately, in recent years many tackle manufacturers have started to produce dual-purpose rods and reels which are suitable both for freshwater work and light sea fishing.

This applies in particular to spinning rods and medium-capacity fixed-spool reels; although it is still a wise precaution to rinse any sort of alloy reel in fresh water after use, even if it does possess a 'sea-proof' specification.

Salmon, pike and carp rods are generally useful for light sea fishing from jetty, rocks, inshore dinghy and sheltered beaches. Coupled with a medium-capacity fixed-spool reel, these rods can be used for quite a variety of methods and species . . . though not of course for tug-of-war tactics with heavy conger and skate.

The small-capacity type of fixed-spool reel used by many freshwater anglers is rather more limited in its scope. It could be used for mulleting and other forms of light float fishing, but would not be much use for dealing with a big bass that was determined to go places.

Hints on choosing a line of suitable strength will be found in Chapter 3. Usually, with the tackle described above, the choice will lie somewhere between 8 lb. and 15 lb. breaking strain, but these limits may have to be varied to suit local shore conditions or the test curve of the rod.

If one took a census of all holiday anglers 'making do' around our coasts with freshwater tackle, it is probable that nine out of ten would be found float fishing from piers, harbour walls and rocks. Those equipped with a roach rod and light quill float often devote their attention to the grey mullet which haunt our estuaries, harbours and inshore rocks.

Thousands of freshwater anglers, who hitherto considered sea fishing a 'chuck it and chance it' business, have been compelled to alter their views after pitting their wits again these wily fish. They are often to be seen cruising slowly to and fro in a harbour or estuary, occasionally rumpling the surface, and at such times they appear to be rather sluggish fish. When hooked, however, they put up a powerful fight, and very often come off best. Being soft mouthed, they must be played and brought to the net very carefully.

Sliding float tackle, using a small drilled float, also provides excellent sport with other species such as pollack, mackerel, bass, wrasse, garfish and scad. (See Chapters 2 and 9.)

However, despite the pleasures of float fishing, it is difficult to understand why so many temporary holiday sea anglers confine themselves to this method. Many of these visitors from inland come equipped with a threadline outfit—so why don't they occasionally try spinning for bass, pollack or mackerel? (See Chapter 4).

Certainly I would recommend any freshwater fisherman who possesses some devon minnows, spoons, wagtails, plugs or deadbait tackles to take a selection with him when holidaying by the sea.

Of course, bass don't always fall to the spinner. Quite frequently they are to be found feeding in the surf.

Sea Fishing with Freshwater Tackle

As already mentioned, in estuaries and on open coasts protected from the prevailing winds, the temporary sea angler should experience little difficulty in shore casting with a salmon, pike or carp rod. On an exposed coast, however, conditions are much less suitable for the use of light tackle; although—contrary to popular belief—they are not impossible unless the surf is really heavy.

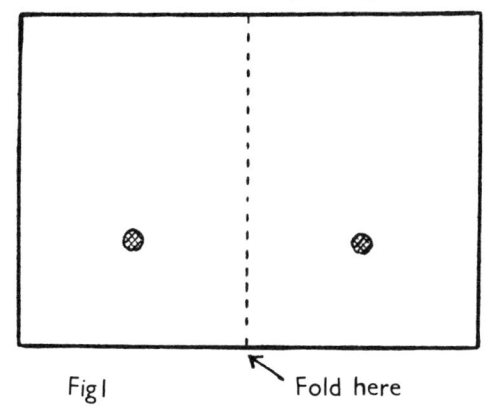

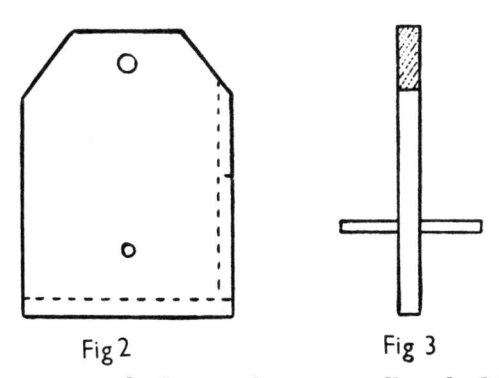

Fig 1   Fold here

Fig 2   Fig 3

Fig. 21. Method of making a small spiked lead.

Two main problems have to be overcome—getting the bait out far enough, and preventing it from being washed back inshore again once it is there.

Using a light line will go a long way towards surmounting both difficulties. It will add distance to one's casts, and offer less resistance to the surge and drag of the surf.

At the same time, though, it must be remembered that a combination of heavy surf and abrasive sand can play havoc with very fine monofilament, so don't be tempted to use a line that is *too* light. It is the last few yards of line which receive most of the wear, and many light shore fishing specialists allow for this by adding about ten yards of slightly heavier line to the end of the main reel line.

If your tackle still gets washed in, on no account try to prevent this happening by using a lead heavier than your rod is designed to cast. Instead, consider whether you are using the most efficient type of lead.

A flat lead naturally grips the sea-bed better than a round one—but a spiked lead is even better. However, spiked leads are rarely made in sizes suitable for casting with light rods, and you will probably have to make your own.

My method is to cut out a rectangle of sheet lead of the desired weight, and then drive 1 in. wire nails through the lead about a quarter of the way across from either side. (See Fig. 21).

The lead is then folded in half like a book, leaving the nails sticking out at either side. These should be nipped off with pliers, so that only ⅜ in. protrudes from the lead. A hole is then drilled through the top of the lead so that it can be attached to the terminal tackle.

To avoid any risk of the lead opening up in use, the sides should be clenched over. A neater job will result if the lead is folded slightly off-centre, and the longer side clenched over the shorter side.

This type of lead is very efficient on a sandy bottom. but it does not hold or wear well on shingle. However, shingle beaches are usually steep-to, and this means that the waves break closer inshore, and the surge and drag of the surf does not have nearly so much effect on the tackle.

It is, of course, the breaking waves which tug most

Sea Fishing with Freshwater Tackle

strongly at the line, and one of the reasons why fairly long rods are favoured by beach fishermen is that they help to hold the line clear of the inshore breakers. The holiday fisherman, making do with a shorter rod, can often use natural features of the foreshore to offset this disadvantage.

For example, exposed shingle beaches usually rise in a series of steep ridges, and by taking up a position at the top of a ridge it is possible to keep the line clear of the worst breakers.

Level sandy shores, on the other hand, are frequently broken up by wave-washed outcrops of rock. These can also provide extra height above the broken water, thereby enabling a light lead to do the same job as a heavier one fished from the open beach.

CHAPTER 6

Prelude to Boat Fishing

BOAT FISHING in salt water falls into two distinct classes—deep-sea fishing in a fair-sized craft; and inshore or estuary fishing, often with a rowing or outboard-powered dinghy, or small motor launch.

Anglers who live some distance inland are usually content to do their deep-sea fishing in a hired craft, under the guidance of an experienced boatman. Inevitably this makes it a rather costly branch of the sport, but many consider that the larger catches so often obtained from deep water justify the extra expense.

There is also a special fascination to be found in deep-sea fishing. It is, I fancy, the dark mystery of all that water under the keel that captures the imagination when we try our luck far offshore. Out beyond the twenty-fathom line we become convinced that anything—literally anything—may suddenly snatch at our line.

At the same time, though, it cannot be denied that deep-sea fishing has its disadvantages. For instance, there is the problem of getting the bait down to the sea-bed in a fairly strong run of tide. A heavy lead is required when a mass of water, 20 fathoms deep, and moving at maybe 2 knots, is pressing against the line and a large almost-buoyant bait.

Even so, the effects of tidal drag do not end there. When a large fish takes the bait, the tide drags on the fish as well; and if it happens to be one of the less streamlined species— a skate, for instance—this tide-resistance can be really formidable.

All this naturally necessitates the use of a fairly heavy, non-stretch line; which in turn results in still more tide-drag. Truly a vicious circle.

Prelude to Boat Fishing

Of course, present-day deep-sea anglers try to fine down their tackle as much as possible, but even so it is still heavy compared with that used by the inshore angler.

As a result, the inshore angler contends that he gets more sport from his modest-sized fish on light tackle, than does the deep-sea enthusiast when playing larger fish on heavier tackle.

Playing a deep-sea fish consists very largely of pumping it up from the depths somewhere more or less directly underneath the boat. For excitement, skill and sport this simply cannot compare with the headlong rush of a large bass over a sand-bar, or the far-weaving antics of a tope taken in shallow water.

Yet again, many big fish taken from deep water have all the fight knocked out of them long before they are brought near the surface, owing to the sudden change in water pressure.

There is, in fact, a good deal to be said for both branches of boat angling, and it is certainly quite wrong to look upon inshore angling as the 'poor relation' of deep-sea fishing.

Realising this, the wise boat angler does not take sides, but samples every kind of fishing the sea has to offer. At neap tides, in settled weather, he visits the outer marks in the hope that some monster of the deep will join him in a saga-making battle.

On other occasions, however, he is equally content to use the greater variety of methods, and the more delicate degrees of rodcraft, that are available to the person who fishes inshore.

Safety Afloat

Inshore sea fishing on the more sheltered types of coast offers the angler a chance of getting afloat without a boatman, and at many popular sea fishing resorts, such as Looe, Fowey and Salcombe (to name just a few in the West Country), it is possible to hire 'self-drive' dinghies and launches. When hired on a weekly basis, and shared by two or three anglers, the cost is very reasonable.

However, even on a sheltered stretch of coast, it is most desirable that anglers going afloat by themselves should know something about boat craft and the ways of the sea. The following list of safety rules should therefore be noted carefully by beginners:

When hiring a dinghy from a reputable boatman you can be reasonably certain that it is in seaworthy condition. Nevertheless, it is always wise to check that there is a bailing can aboard, and that the oars and rowlocks are beyond reproach.

Don't put all your faith in a motor, whether inboard or outboard. Carry oars always, and never venture under power into any situation from which you cannot extricate yourself by rowing, should the necessity arise.

If the weather is at all unsettled, it is a wise plan to choose a fishing mark that is upwind of your starting point. Then, if the wind freshens, it will help you to get back to base in a hurry.

In adopting this precaution, however, don't allow yourself to become over-confident. Winds do sometimes change direction at very short notice.

Along certain coasts, where tides run strongly, the direction of the currents may be a more important consideration than the direction of the wind; although neither factor should be neglected.

Ideally, one's line of retreat should be with both wind and tide, and arranging this is very largely a matter of timing. In the majority of coastal waters the tidal flow changes direction about every six hours, and although this rhythm is directly related to the times of high and low water on shore, the relationship varies from coast to coast.

For example, in an estuary slack water usually coincides with high or low water, but in the open sea outside the estuary the coastwise currents may well be running at their maximum velocity at high and low water.

An Admiralty chart—which should be regarded as a 'must' by every serious boat angler—will enable you to forecast accurately the speed and direction of flow of local

Prelude to Boat Fishing

tidal currents at any hour of the day.

Another point which needs to be borne in mind is that 'wind against tide' results in an unpleasant sea. Thus, when the tidal current changes direction, the wave-action may quite suddenly alter from an easy rolling swell to an ugly prancing lop.

These conditions are usually most noticeable off headlands, in the mouths of exposed estuaries, and over rocky marks or steep ridges on the sea-bed. Some headlands, too, are beset by a collision of currents, resulting in a 'race' which can, in certain cases, spell disaster for even sizable craft.

The Portland Race, off the Dorset coast, is a classic example. There the tide at Springs flows at over seven knots, and large mushroom-shaped waves—every one a potential 'swamper'—leap into the air.

Large waves and heavy swells also become dangerous in any area where the water shallows—over sandbars, reefs, or close inshore. This is because the reduced depth of water tends to 'trip up' the waves, so that they become very steep, and then topple over in a smother of surf. A small boat which gets among these breakers could very easily capsize.

Of all the hidden dangers which lie in wait for the novice boatman, however, it is the offshore wind which claims most victims every summer. An offshore wind means a calm sea close inshore—as calm, very often, as the proverbial millpond.

For the amateur sea-dog, venturing forth in a small pulling dinghy, this following wind makes the voyage out to sea very pleasant and easy. Only when he is well out of the shelter of land, and the millpond has been transformed into a flurry of chop-licking whitecaps, does he suddenly realise his danger.

Putting about, he begins rowing for the distant shore. It is then that he learns what an exhausting business it is, trying to make headway with oars against a strong wind and a breaking sea!

Anchors and Killicks

As a safeguard against being carried into a dangerous situation by strong winds or currents, every boat should carry an anchor. In fact, experienced boat anglers often carry two kinds of anchoring device.

One of these usually consists of a heavy iron or concrete weight, known as a killick, for use over rocky fishing marks where it would be unwise to risk anything more elaborate.

A killick, however, will not hold a boat over a sandy or shingly sea-bed when it is being hard-pressed by waves, wind or tide. For this sort of situation a *properly designed* fluked anchor should be carried, of adequate holding power to meet any emergency.

An anchor must be given plenty of rope if the flukes are to bite home properly. The general rule is to allow three fathoms of rope for every fathom of water. It will also be found that this length of rope allows the boat to ride the waves with a much easier motion.

A fathom or two of chain shackled on between the anchor and the rope will help to weigh down the shank and stock. In this way the drag exerted on the anchor is much closer to the horizontal, and the flukes bite home more quickly.

There are other advantages, too, in having a short length of chain next to the anchor. The most obvious one is that it prevents the anchor rope coming into contact with sea-bed rocks, and possibly fraying through.

Another advantage will not make itself apparent until one day you try to drop anchor in fairly deep water when your boat is drifting fast before a strong wind. If the anchor is of a light dinghy pattern, and attached direct to a rope without any chain, the chances are that it will stream away in the water like a trolling lure without making contact with the bottom at all.

Of course, this difficulty can be overcome by turning the boat into the wind, either with the motor or oars. But if your boat is out of control for any reason—with engine trouble or a broken oar, maybe—then your anchor is going to be useless just when you need it most.

Prelude to Boat Fishing

The question of which type of anchor is most suitable for the angler is not an easy one to answer.

The Admiralty pattern is quite reliable for casual anchoring while fishing, but the business of knocking in the pin wastes valuable seconds in an emergency.

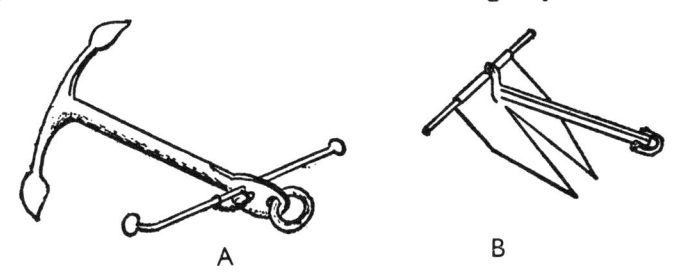

Fig. 22. Two types of anchor. A—"Fisherman" type, B—Stockless type.

The patent stockless anchors are more compact, are ready for use at a moment's notice, and cannot become fouled by the rope when the boat swings to the tide. Not all of them, however, lend themselves to being 'tripped'.

Tripping an anchor is a precaution against losing it should one of the flukes become wedged under a rock or other obstruction. The rope or chain is attached first of all to the *crown* of the anchor, and is then brought up the shank and hitched to the normal attachment eye by means of a piece of cord which will break under a hefty pull.

Thus, under ordinary fishing conditions, the anchor will hold the boat. If it becomes jammed, however, a strong, sharp pull when the rope is vertical will break the tripping cord, and the pull will immediately be transferred to the crown, and the fluke will be drawn clear of the obstruction.

It must be stressed, though, that an anchor tripped by this method should only be used for fishing. It must never be used for anchoring a boat that is to be left unattended overnight.

Locating Fishing Marks

Boat anglers are nearly always ready to argue about the best ways of catching fish. On one point, however, all are agreed—that to catch fish one must first of all know where to seek them. In other words, it pays to 'know the marks'.

However, there is nothing mysterious about this business of knowing where certain species of fish are likely to be found. Local knowledge certainly does count for a lot, but at the same time there are many ways in which the visiting angler, experienced in handling a boat, may enjoy good fishing on marks of his own discovering.

There are, of course, an infinite variety of fishing marks, each with its own minor peculiarities. For our purpose, however, we can divide them conveniently into the following groups:

(a) Extensive submerged reefs, which may or may not be marked by isolated rocks showing above the surface of the sea, or by a bell buoy or similar navigational warning. (Fish which may be expected: pollack, wrasse, conger, huss, coalfish, pouting).

(b) Isolated rocks, surrounded by sand or mud. (Conger, possibly pollack and wrasse when the rocks cover a moderately wide area; bream in weedy areas; flatfish and gurnard on soft ground fringing the mark).

(c) Broken ground, i.e. small rocks scattered thickly among sand, grit, shingle or mud, with here and there a larger mass of seaweedy rock. (Skate, conger, pollack, coalfish, pouting, huss, and possibly a roving bass. Bream may also be found over weedy marks).

(d) Areas of fine sand, fine sand mixed with shell grit, or muddy sand. (Plaice, dabs, turbot, lesser spotted dogfish, tope, smooth hound, and whiting in season).

(e) Areas of shingle and coarse sand. (Not as a rule very productive. Possibly a few dabs, poor cod and lesser spotted dogfish).

(f) Areas of mud and ooze. (Not very productive in the open sea, unless the mud harbours marine worms or burrowing molluscs, when flatfish and their predators will be present. Flounders, bass and mullet in or near estuaries).

(g) Submerged sand-bars near river-mouth. (Bass, dabs, plaice, and possibly tope in season).

Prelude to Boat Fishing

(h) Sand banks in the open sea. (Plaice, turbot, lesser spotted dogfish, smooth hound, possibly tope in season).
(i) Sounds, estuary and sea-loch narrows, and other 'bottlenecks' through which fish moving from one area to another are likely to pass. (All roving species, whether bottom feeders or otherwise).

With the above information at his disposal, the first job of the angler must obviously be to survey the local inshore waters. To simplify this task, Ernest Benn Ltd publish a series of inexpensive booklets which give details and chart the positions of all the boat and shore fishing marks along the south coast. At the time of writing those dealing with the sea fishing in Somerset, Devon, Cornwall, Dorset, Hampshire, Sussex and Kent have already been published.

In other areas an Admiralty chart will be of considerable help, especially if the area is well frequented by shipping, and is therefore covered by one of the larger-scale sheets.

The general nature of the sea-bed will be indicated (i.e. sand, rock, shell, mud, etc.); while isolated rocks, reefs and sand banks will be pinpointed with a note of their depth.

However, the information given by the chart will, in many instances, amount to little more than a clue on which the angler will have to do some hard and thoughtful detective work. For example, if you are seeking a good plaice mark, you will have to hunt around in a sandy area, taking samples of the sea-bed with a plummet loaded with grease.

In due course you may strike a bank or hollow of fine bright sand, well mixed with broken shell. This will point to an abundance of shellfish down below, and as plaice are attracted to such areas the killick will be lowered and the spot tested with suitable baits and tackle.

If the place proves rewarding, its position should be pin-pointed by taking compass bearings, or by noting two pairs of aligned landmarks on the shore. Remember, though, that you may wish to find the spot again in hazy weather or at dusk, so don't choose landmarks that are too far distant.

Complete Guide to Sea Fishing

Now let us take a look at what are sometimes called 'hard-bottom marks'—areas of broken ground and rock.

In some ways, a large-scale chart is even more useful for this aspect of mark-hunting, because the limits of rocks and reefs are usually plotted much more meticulously by the Admirality survey authorities than soft-bottom areas.

Fig. 23. Plummet for taking samples of the sea-bed.

The reason for this, of course, is that rocks are liable to foul anchors, and are consequently always a bit of a menace to the mariner, whatever the depth of the water.

Areas of sand or mud, on the other hand, only concern the average navigator when they rise too close to the surface.

By studying a large-scale chart, therefore, and noting the configuration of the coastline, the position of prominent landmarks, etc., it is often possible to work out a pair of cross-bearings for a rock mark before actually setting out on a fishing trip.

Indeed, Trinity House may even have saved you the trouble by marking the reef with a buoy if it constitutes a menace to shipping. In this case, however, bear in mind that the buoy will not be directly over the reef, but will probably lie a hundred yards or more to seaward of it.

The chart will tell you exactly how far, and you should head in from the buoy on a compass bearing until you are over the mark. Your plummet (or echo-sounder, if you

Prelude to Boat Fishing

have one) will tell you when you are over rock.

In some areas—as, for example, off Cornwall—many submerged rocks are very tall and steep-to, so that the depth may suddenly decrease from maybe 30 fathoms to less than 10 fathoms. As a rule it is best to fish close beside these outcrops, in deep water, not on top of them in shallow water.

If you don't possess a chart, there are plenty of other ways of locating the haunts of rock fish. It is useful to remember, for instance, that rocky stretches of coast are often matched by corresponding areas of rock out at sea.

Thus, off a rugged headland one will nearly always locate a submerged reef—possibly running well out into deep water.

The whereabouts of other patches of rock will often be indicated by streamers of lobster-pot corks; while if you are of the stuff that pioneers are made of, and wish to discover a virgin fishing ground, this can often be done by *slowly* trailing a chunk of metal, about 4 or 5 lb. in weight, along the sea-bed until you meet an obstruction. Don't use a grapnel, because the flukes will almost certainly become hopelessly snagged.

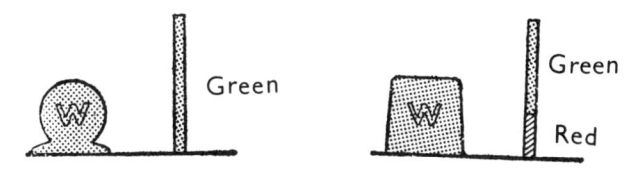

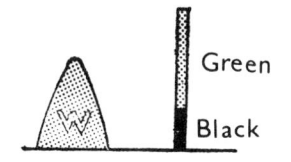

Fig. 24. Three types of wreck buoys.

Complete Guide to Sea Fishing

Sunken vessels also provide excellent and often very interesting fishing. These are best located with the aid of an echo-sounder; although it is usually necessary to refer to a chart in the first instance to obtain bearings on the approximate locality.

It is an odd fact that wrecks are often grouped on the sea-bed in pairs or clusters. Possibly they are the result of collisions, or attacks upon convoys by aircraft or U-boats. Whatever the reason, these wreck groupings certainly do increase one's chances of locating a wreck without too much delay.

Of course, if the wreck is in shallow water, or in a sheltered bay commonly used as an anchorage, its position may be marked by a buoy or spar. Wreck buoys are painted green, and it is worth noting that the shape (or colour-system in the case of spars) indicates the wreck's position in relation to the buoy.

Boating the Fish

Good fish are all too often lost through lack of a gaff or landing net.

A gaff for boat fishing should be needle-sharp and really strong; for there is always the chance of hooking an outsize skate or conger. In particular, the gaff-head should be very firmly attached to the handle. A satisfactory gaff-hook for general boat fishing is the inexpensive lash-on type fitted with an out-jutting tongue of metal at the top of the shank. This tongue, or tang as it is sometimes called, fits into a hole in the handle, and prevents the hook from being wrenched off by the twisting and thrashing of a big fish.

It is a good idea, after lashing on a gaff hook with strong twine, to reinforce it with a narrow lashing of strong copper wire on either side of the twine. This will act as a safeguard should the twine lashing, through an oversight, be allowed to become rotten and weak.

A landing net for sea fishing should have a large frame, preferably galvanised to resist the corrosive action of salt water. Folding frames are not recommended.

Prelude to Boat Fishing

Alternatively, a perfectly good frame can be made out of a Y-shaped fork of ash, cut from a growing tree. Seasoned, and painted a dull blue or green (to avoid scaring the hooked fish), this will last for a great many years, and there will be no metal parts to rust and cause damage to the netting.

CHAPTER 7

Boat Fishing at Anchor

AS mentioned in the previous chapter, many kinds of fish tend to congregate near rocks, sunken wrecks and various other marks covering a limited area of the sea-bed. When fishing these places it is often convenient to anchor the boat, using one of the following methods:

BOTTOM FISHING

The Paternoster (see Fig. 9) is much used by sea anglers when fishing for ground-feeding species from an anchored boat. The modern trend is to use inconspicuous traces made up at home from nylon monofilament, but *occasionally* when tides are slack, and there is not enough current to stream the baited hooks away from the trace, it may be an advantage to use a paternoster fitted with out-jutting booms.

These booms are often made of brass or stainless steel wire. The brass types are to be preferred, because they quickly become tarnished when used in salt water, and are then much less likely to scare fish than those made of shiny stainless steel.

Still more inconspicuous, however, are the 'invisible' booms of transparent celluloid, which can be threaded on to a monofilament trace. These are particularly suitable for whiting, and other small to medium-sized species.

Although paternoster tackle is normally used close to the bottom, it is not often allowed to lie on the sea-bed beneath a slack line. The most common method is to lower the tackle to the bottom, and then reel it up again for a foot or two, so that it is suspended clear of rocks and weed.

However, there are exceptions. For instance, when fishing in a shallow estuary or bay, fish would probably be

Boat Fishing at Anchor

deterred from approaching a bait suspended only a couple of fathoms below the boat. Under these circumstances a light monofilament paternoster is often cast out so that it rests on the bottom some distance away from the boat. Needless to say, this is only practicable when the bottom is reasonably free from snags—and crabs!

Most paternosters used from a boat carry either two or three hooks, so an important advantage of this type of tackle is that different hook sizes and baits can be presented at the same time—thus increasing the prospects of a mixed bag. Another advantage, when the paternoster is suspended on a tight line, is that the baited hooks, streaming out at intervals on the vertical trace, search more than one depth.

Paternoster tackle is often used when boat fishing for bream, cod, pouting, whiting and wrasse, but is capable of catching many other species, including flatfish, when allowed to lie on the sea-bed. However, when it is desired to place baits on the sea-bed, it is usually better to use a paternoster-trot (see Fig. 10), or the leger tackle described below.

The Free-Running Leger (see Fig. 11) is used with the lead resting on the bottom. The reel line, which runs freely through a hole or eye in the lead, is kept fairly taut, but when fishing for certain species, such as tope or conger, the reel is often checked by finger pressure only, or a feather-light touch of the drag. Thus, when a fish moves off with the bait, the line is able to run out freely without the fish feeling any resistance from the lead or reel.

Legering is a pleasant method of bottom fishing, because it provides good sport even when sea conditions make it essential to use a heavy lead. When boat fishing it is used mainly to catch conger, dogfish, skate, tope, flatfish, large cod, haddock and (in estuaries) ground-feeding bass.

The main disadvantage of this type of tackle is that the trace is liable to become caught up when the sea-bed is snaggy; although this difficulty can be overcome to a certain extent by weighting the tackle so that the line goes down steeply with a minimum of 'tide-slant'.

Although legering is primarily a means of taking those fish which actually feed on the sea-bed, the method can be modified so that the bait is presented a foot or two above the bottom. This is done by suspending the running lead on about 24 inches of line; the other end of the line being attached to a swivel threaded on the main reel line.

This idea can be particularly useful when the sea-bed is weedy, and it is desired to present the bait above the weeds.

The short length of line should possess a lower breaking strain than the main reel line, so that only the lead will be lost if it becomes caught up in the weeds.

DRIFTLINING

In recent years the driftline method of fishing has become increasingly popular with boat and pier anglers. This is hardly surprising, because it fits in ideally with the present-day trend towards light sea tackle and lively rods. Also, it is capable of catching a wide range of fish, and enables maximum sport to be obtained with such species as bass, pollack, mackerel and black bream.

The principle of the driftline is simplicity itself. A single baited hook is allowed to stream away from the fishing position on the tide, and the depth at which the bait is presented is controlled by the amount of lead on the line.

As slack water approaches (approximately every six hours in most places) the tidal flow will gradually decrease until it may be possible to dispense with lead altogether. Similarly, even when there is a fair run of tide, lead is often unnecessary when trying for fish which are feeding very close to the surface.

When driftlining it is, of course, necessary to anchor the boat up-tide of the mark, but the actual distance varies according to the species sought and depth of water. In the case of pollack, bream, wrasse and pouting, the reel line is usually weighted so that it slants down fairly steeply,

Boat Fishing at Anchor

until it terminates in a 4-5 ft. trace flowing freely in the tide.

When fishing for such fish as bass, mackerel and garfish, however, the line is often allowed to slant away much more gradually, so that the bait may be fished 75 yards or more astern of the boat. Because there is little risk of these species going to ground among rocks, it is also possible to use a much longer trace. This is unlikely to improve your catch of mackerel, but very often it does help considerably to lull the suspicions of bass.

Provided there are no wrasse-inhabited rocks nearby, I often have 15 yards of line between the lead and hook when driftlining for bass. This is fairly common practice in the West Country. Of course, to avoid the lead jamming against the rod end-ring when reeling in, it is necessary to use a sliding lead with some sort of automatic release device.

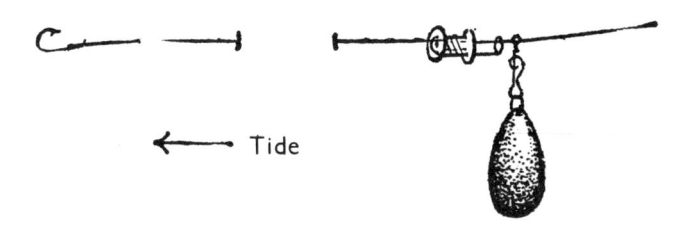

Fig. 25. Driftline fitted with automatic lead release.

In order to derive the maximum amount of pleasure from driftlining, there are several things to aim at when making up the tackle.

As little lead as possible should be used—unless, for the tactical reasons already mentioned, it is desired to fish 'deep and steep'. This is because a heavy lead increases the amount of sag between the horizontal and slanting sections of the line, making it difficult to strike quickly and efficiently. Also, this line-sag tends to 'cushion' the fighting power of the fish.

The effects of line-sag can be reduced by using a fairly short trace, and this is one reason why I do not recommend anything longer than 4-5 ft. when fishing deep for pollack and wrasse. Another reason is that a very long trace would probably allow these fish to dive downwards among the sea-bed rocks.

Many baits can be used for driftlining. Sandeels and prawns, with plenty of wriggle and kick in them, are excellent for bass, pollack and many other species. Ragworm and fish strips are also useful.

Even when using a vigorous livebait it sometimes helps to reel the bait repeatedly and very slowly up through the appropriate fishing depth. This can be particularly effective when after pollack, bream, pouting and other bottom species. Don't stop retrieving if you feel a tentative pluck at the bait. Continue to draw the bait slowly away from the fish, and the movement may be just sufficient to induce it to make a more determined grab.

FLOAT FISHING

Sometimes bass, pollack and various other fish are encountered in rocky coves and creeks, where the absence of any true run of tide makes driftlining impossible. Under these circumstances float tackle, as suggested for pier and rock fishing in Chapter 2, can often be used with success.

RODS AND REELS

Various types of rod are used for boat fishing at anchor, depending upon the methods used, species sought, depth of water, and strength of the local tides. As mentioned in Chapter 6, when fishing in deep water and strong tides it is necessary to use a heavy lead—perhaps weighing as much as 1-1½ lb. This naturally calls for a strong and fairly stiff rod which will not bend too much under the weight of the lead and drag of the tide.

Deep-sea rods used for large skate must be particularly powerful, because these fish are notorious rod-breakers. But for most other species (with the obvious exception of tunny, *large* shark and outsize conger) a 7-8 ft. medium

Boat Fishing at Anchor

boat rod will prove suitable, combining adequate strength with sufficient liveliness to provide enjoyable sport.

For certain boat fishing methods, in fact, it is possible to use quite a light rod—even in deep water. Deep driftlining for bream is one example.

Inshore and estuary anglers will also find many uses for a light rod when legering, driftlining and float fishing.

When estuary fishing with a light rod for bass, flounders, plaice, etc., some dinghy anglers use a medium-capacity fixed-spool reel. For the general run of boat fishing, however, it is customary to use a strong multiplier or centre-pin reel. When deep-water fishing, or streaming a driftline well astern of the boat, it is important to have a reel which holds an adequate amount of line, and is capable of recovering it quickly.

The strength of the line should match the test curve of the rod (see Chapter 3); while for deep-sea fishing it is generally advisable to use a non-stretch line of braided terylene. However, in areas where the tidal currents run fast, nylon monofilament may be more satisfactory despite its elasticity, owing to the fact that its smoother surface reduces tide-drag to a minimum. Wire line (see Chapter 1) is also worth considering when fishing a deep mark where tides run fast.

GROUNDBAITING

When fishing at anchor, catches are often improved by suspending at the fishing depth a weighted and perforated canister containing minced-up mackerel, pilchards and other oily fish. Alternatively, the container can be hitched a fathom or two up the anchor rope. It should not be allowed to rest on the sea-bed, however; otherwise it may attract bait-robbing crabs and starfish.

CHAPTER 8

Boat Fishing Under Way

FISHING from a moving or drifting boat is often resorted to when the fishing ground covers a wide area, or the fish being sought are nomadic in habit. The methods used are as follows:

TROLLING

Trolling, or whiffing as it is known in Cornwall, consists of trailing a natural bait or artificial lure behind a moving boat, and the fish most commonly caught are mackerel, bass, pollack and coalfish. First of all let us consider the tackle required.

The rod should not be too long; otherwise it will soon become tiring to hold when trolling under power for fast-swimming species, owing to the constant water-drag on line, lead and bait. It should also be stiff enough to stand up to this water-drag without bending, and to enable the hook to be driven home firmly when striking a fish.

However, though stiffish, the rod should certainly not be rigid. In fact, quite a light and lively rod can be used when trolling with oars, because then the boat can be allowed to drift while playing a fish.

The reel should carry plenty of line, possess a good recovery rate, and be fitted with an optional check or drag. A medium-capacity multiplier is the popular choice with most sea anglers when trolling under power.

The line should be as fine as can be used with safety, thereby reducing water friction, and so enabling the smallest possible lead and a reasonably light rod to be used. Many use nylon monofilament for this purpose, and it is certainly true that this type of line reduces water-drag to a minimum. On the other hand its habit of stretching

Boat Fishing Under Way

under strain makes it difficult to strike firmly when the bait is being streamed a long way astern of the boat.

A braided terylene line will not stretch nearly so much, and when trolling slowly with a rowing boat this advantage more than offsets the slight increase in water-drag.

However, when trolling under power at anything faster than slow walking speed, water-drag becomes a much more important factor, while the ability to strike firmly decreases slightly in importance, because then the fish quite often hook themselves.

Leads should for preference be of a quick-change pattern, so that the trolling depth can be altered without delay. Spiral leads are commonly used, and these cannot be faulted when fishing for mackerel, pollack and coalfish. When trolling for bass, however, it is sometimes desirable to use a very long trace, and this necessitates the use of a 'release' lead which automatically slides down the line, out of the way of the rod, when retrieving.

Whenever possible it is advisable to incorporate some form of anti-kink device when making up terminal tackle for trolling. A spiral lead, bent slightly between fingers and thumb, and fitted just above the trace swivel, will prevent twist creeping up the reel line.

Of course, this can only be done when using a trace that is no longer than the rod itself, and to prevent a really long flowing trace from twisting it may sometimes be necessary to fit an anti-kink head lead to the front of a lure or bait mount. Choose one with a streamlined shape, so that it will not create an air bubble likely to arouse the suspicions of the fish.

Alternatively, there are plenty of trolling-cum-spinning lures which possess some form of built-in anti-kink device. The popular feathered squid, easily made up at home, is one example.

Lures and Baits. On many parts of the coast the most killing trolling lure for bass is an artificial plastic sandeel. There are several patterns to choose from, but my own favourite is the 'Red Gill'. Available in several colours and two sizes, this plastic sandeel has a very lifelike swimming action, and is readily taken by bass, pollack, mackerel and coalfish. One particularly useful feature of this lure is that it wriggles through the water, but does not spin, and is therefore unlikely to put any kinks in the line.

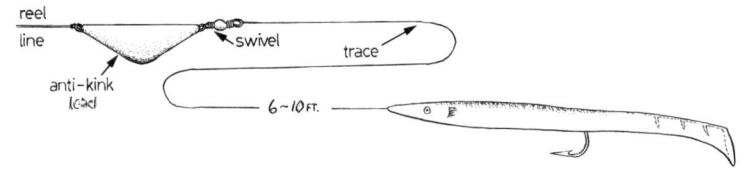

Fig. 26. 'Red Gill' plastic sandeel.

Next in popularity comes the rubber tube-bait. This is not so good for mackerel, but it can be a killer for pollack and bass. Red, amber and green seem to be the best colours for pollack, but the most effective colours for bass vary from district to district. Yellow, amber, red, silver, white and black are all capable of producing good results.

No artificial sandeel is half so effective as a live one, however, and this should be trolled slowly and quietly on a long flowing trace, so that it is free to swim and wriggle as attractively as possible.

Although a dead sandeel does not make such a good bait as a live one, it is still quite useful when trolled because the movement helps to give it the appearance of being alive.

Preserved sandeels vary in their effectiveness according to the preserving method used. Many do quite well at times, though fish tend to ignore them when shoals of live sandeels are plentiful.

Baited-spoon fishing is simply another form of trolling when it is carried on from a moving boat. The method is best known as a means of catching flounders (see Chapter 9), and it is not so widely realised that a baited spoon will also catch bass and other fish. Good results with bass up to 8 lb. or more have been obtained with a plain 1½ in. silver spoon terminating in a ragworm-baited Pennell tackle. (See Fig. 27).

Boat Fishing Under Way

Trolling Techniques

Success in trolling depends upon fishing (i) at the right depth, (ii) in the right place, (iii) at the right speed, (iv) at the right time, and (v) with the right tackle, bait and/or lure.

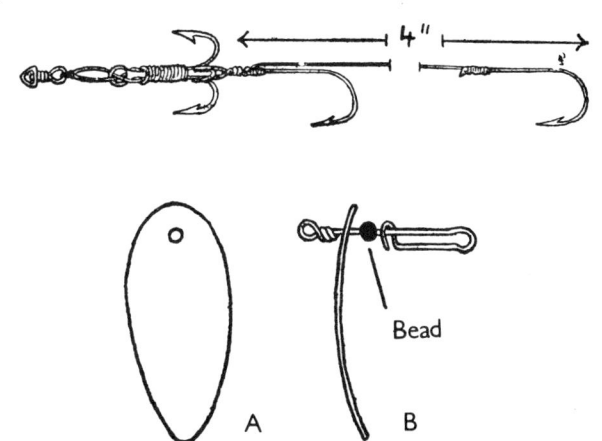

Fig. 27. Baited spoon tackle for bass. A—Outline of spoon, B—Mounted spoon clips on to trace swivel.

Flounders, needless to say, are taken by trolling near the bottom. So are pollack as a rule, although around dawn or dusk they often rise towards the surface. This is, in fact, the best time to troll for pollack—partly because they are usually in an obliging mood then, and partly because there is not so much risk of snagging tackle among the sea-bed rocks and weeds.

Incidentally, a fluorescent lure will be found very useful for trolling in the half-light of dawn or dusk.

The swimming depth of bass is variable. Much depends upon what these fish happen to be feeding on at the time, and the overall depth of the water. As a rule, however, one does not expect to troll very deep for bass, nor very far from the shore. In particular, tidal estuaries are favoured by this species.

Mackerel are usually located about 6 ft. to 20 ft. deep, and their interest is stimulated by a fast-moving bait.

Bass also take fast-moving baits, although one of the most killing methods for this species is slow drift-trolling with a live bait. This is best carried out with a light pulling dinghy, the angler giving a quiet pull at the oars every few seconds to keep the bait streamed astern. For preference, the rowing direction should be *across* the tide.

The best bait for drift-trolling is live sandeel, but live prawn and ragworm are also good. When using ragworm, a baby spinner or piece of aluminium foil mounted above the hook helps a lot.

Although some readers will probably disagree with me, I consider this method much more pleasant than trolling under power. However, if it is to be enjoyed properly the dinghy *must* be light and easy to row—which means fishing alone without a bulky passenger sitting in the stern!

Single-handed trolling is a lot easier than many people imagine. The first thing to do is to arrange some means of propping the rod up in the boat. If you own your own dinghy, I suggest you fit it with the detachable rod rest and butt-socket shown in Fig. 28.

When rowboat trolling it is important to guard against snagging the bottom. Start off by allowing only a fathom or two of line to run into the water; then apply the reel check and place the rod in the rest and socket. Take a few pulls at the oars, and, when fairly under way, release the check. The line will then run off the reel and stream astern.

If you think the reel is running too fast, so that the lead is sinking too deep for safety, tighten the drag adjustment slightly.

Oars do not scare fish to nearly the same extent as a motor, and even for bass it is generally unnecessary to stream out more than 60-75 yards of line. When the desired amount has run off, flick the reel into gear but slacken the drag sufficiently to prevent the rod being pulled overboard when a big fish takes the lure. On getting a bite, give one more hard pull on the oars to drive the hook into the fish; then quickly slide your oars inboard through the rowlocks, and pick up the rod.

Restrain your fish, but make no attempt to recover line

Boat Fishing Under Way

until all way has fallen off the boat. Then, if your previous experience of trolling has been limited to heavy motor boats, with heavy tackle to match, you are due for a big surprise.

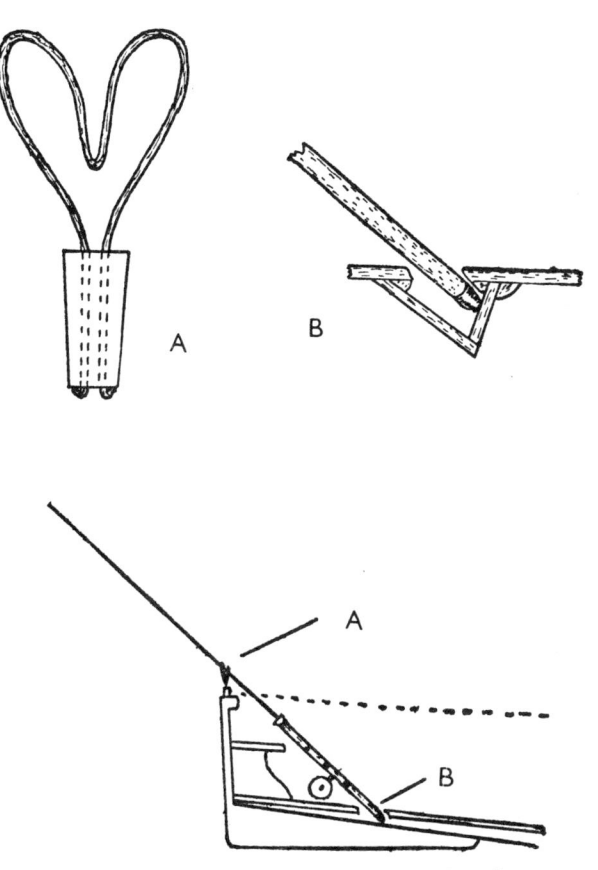

Figs. 28 and 28a. Rod rest for dinghy.

One final word of warning. Remember that wind and tide may take charge of the boat while you are busy with the fish. So if you have been trolling near rocks, and the tussle looks like lasting several minutes, it may be advisable to throw the killick overboard.

Certainly, when trolling single-handed, some form of anchoring device should always be kept handy for immediate use, with the end of the rope already made fast to a cleat.

DRIFT-FISHING AND DRAG-LINING

The term 'drift-fishing' means drifting before the wind or tide with a baited hook suspended *above* the sea-bed. 'Drag-lining' is similar to drift-fishing, except that—as the name implies—the bait is dragged or tripped *along* the sea-bed.

In the case of drift-fishing, the level at which the hook is suspended depends upon the species one is seeking. Over extensive rocky areas it can be a rewarding method of taking pollack, and is then often combined with a sink and retrieve technique.

Within reason, the bait can be sunk as fast as you like, but reeling in should be done slowly. Normally you will contact the pollack within the first twenty feet above the rocks, although this is not a hard and fast rule. Obviously, when sinking the bait you must be careful not to send it down too far to a snaggy end among the rocks, and one way to prevent this happening (if you are using braided line) is to mark the line at intervals with indelible ink.

Drift-fishing possesses several advantages, and an important one is the fact that boat and tide are usually travelling in the same direction, and at approximately the same speed. This means that very little lead need be used to sink the bait—which in turn offers an opportunity to use a light and sporting rod even when fishing in deep water.

Another advantage of drift-fishing is that a wide area is covered, and in this way there is a good chance of discovering places which provide an above-average yield of fish.

Drag-lining, of course, can be carried on only over snag-free areas of sea-bed, although in some places, where conditions permit, some very good catches of plaice are taken by drag-lining over sandy or shelly ground bordering rocks. Needless to say, accurate local knowledge is needed for this sort of fishing.

Boat Fishing Under Way

The tackle for drag-lining may be either some form of single-hook leger, or—where whiting are present—a two-hook paternoster. In the latter case the top hook is baited for whiting, and is mounted on a 6 in. dropper in the usual way. The lower hook, however, is tied to a 4 ft. length of monofilament so that the bait trails along, or very close to, the sea-bed.

Drag-lining is also capable of providing good catches of flounders in snag-free estuaries. One important advantage is that robber-crabs—so often troublesome in estuaries—do not have a chance to get their claws on the moving bait.

Dragging weight
Tide
Fig 1

Sea anchor
Fig 2

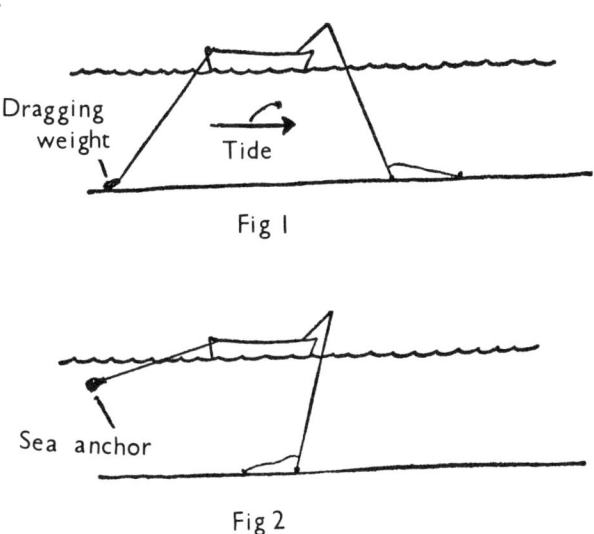

Fig. 29. Methods of checking a drifting boat.

Two things may make drift-fishing or drag-lining difficult—too much wind or too swift a tide. When either of these make the boat drift too fast, there is a probability that you will lose contact with whiting and other shoal fish almost as soon as they are found; although a rubby-dubby net suspended at the fishing depth sometimes encourages them to keep tagging along.

Also, although a moving bait has a definite attraction for flounders, plaice and turbot, the movement must not be *too* fast.

The usual remedy when the drift is caused by the tide is to drag a weight along the sea-bed, thereby slowing down the boat without stopping it altogether.

When checking wind-drift, however, you will probably spoil your fishing if you drag a weight along the bottom, because the baited tackle will then be slanting the opposite way. (See illustration). Instead, it is better to trail some crude form of sea anchor, such as a bunched sack or wicker basket at the end of a rope.

FEATHERING

Feathering, or 'fishing the feathers' as it is sometimes called, consists of working a trace of feathered hooks with a slow up-and-down jigging motion—usually from a drifting boat, or while moving very slowly under power.

Commercial handliners, using traces carrying as many as two dozen hooks, frequently make very large catches of mackerel and pollack by this method. Rod and reel anglers, however, would be well advised to restrict themselves to shorter traces carrying not more than seven hooks—and even with this number it will be necessary to use a stiff conger rod, or something similar. This is because one has to use a very heavy lead with these feathered traces, and when a shoal of mackerel is struck it is by no means unusual to catch a fish on every hook.

This is undoubtedly a quick method of catching one's supper, or a supply of bait, but it can hardly be called angling. If sport is the prime object, it is far better to limit the number of feathered hooks to three, so that a lighter lead and a lively rod can be used.

Even with this modified tackle it is possible to make surprisingly large catches.

It is possible to make a feathered trace, using tinned haddock hooks, a cockerel's hackle feathers, and strong nylon monofilament. As a general rule, however, the beginner will be well advised to buy a professionally tied

Boat Fishing Under Way

trace from his tackle dealer. When attaching this to the line, care should be taken to fit it the right way up.

To avoid tangles when several fish are caught at a time, bring the trace inboard but hold it up so that it remains taut. Then begin unhooking the fish from the top, working downwards.

SPINNING

Spinning from the shore has already been dealt with at length in Chapter 4, and it is only necessary to mention here that the same method can be used very successfully from a drifting boat.

Pollack and bass are often taken by drifting and spinning around wave-washed rocks; mackerel and bass by quietly approaching shoals of whitebait, sprats and other small fry upon which the larger fish are likely to be feeding.

The presence of one of these shoals is often revealed by the activities of sea-birds. If the fry are near the surface, gulls will be excitedly wheeling and diving upon them, and this will tell the angler that the bass or mackerel are also probably near the surface.

On the other hand, the presence of razorbills and guillemots, instead of gulls, usually indicates that the fry—and therefore the larger fish—are swimming fairly deep.

During the summer (June to September) drift-spinning for shoaling bass is often very good in large estuaries, particularly in the early morning before the fish have been disturbed by boat traffic. When approaching a shoal it is advisable to do so from an up-wind or an up-tide direction. This will enable you to cut off the motor while still some distance away, making the final approach by rowing or quietly drifting down on the fish.

A sandbar near the mouth of an estuary is often a favourite shoaling area for bass, especially during the early flood tide.

CHAPTER 9

Sea Fish A.B.C.

IN the following pages will be found an alphabetical list of those fish taken on rod and line around the coasts of Britain. The information given includes a description of most species, together with details of its haunts and feeding habits, and the tackle, methods and baits used to catch it.

Those fish marked with a star (*) are of particular interest to the angler, and for this reason they have been dealt with at greater length than the less sporting species.

ANGLER FISH

Haunts: Spends most of its time lying on the sea-bed, usually on muddy sand, close to weedy rocks. It is able to change colour to blend with its surroundings, and is rendered even more inconspicuous by some weed-like pieces of skin growing around its body and lower jaws.

Feeding Habits: The angler fish derives its name from the fact that it 'fishes' for its food. The first ray of its dorsal fin is prolonged to such an extent that it overhangs its enormous mouth, and at the end of this 'rod' there is a brightly coloured lure. When the angler fish sees a small pouting or some other likely victim, it twitches the lure to and fro, and in this way the smaller fish, filled with curiosity, is enticed just a little too close to the large open mouth!

Fishing Methods: The angler fish is only occasionally caught on rod and line—usually with a large fish bait presented on ground tackle. If you do happen to hook one, beware of its dangerous jaws, which in a split second can snap shut on a carelessly placed hand or foot.

Sea Fish A. B. C.

° BASS

No fish is more highly prized by British sea anglers than the bass. A decent-sized specimen makes a powerful, slashing bite at the bait, and when hooked it usually runs far and fast, scorning to go to ground among rocks. In colour it is a deep bluish-grey on the back, shading to silvery on the sides. British rod-caught record: 18 lb. 2 oz. (Felixstowe Beach, 1943).

Location and Season: Bass are encountered mainly around the southern halves of England and Ireland, and around the Welsh coast. The majority are captured from late Spring until late Autumn, but in some localities (notably in Cornwall and South Devon) they often remain inshore throughout most of the winter.

Haunts: Bass are very largely an inshore fish, and are commonly found in estuaries, over shoals, in coves and surf-swept bays, and in the vicinity of rocky headlands. They are powerful, restless fish, and have a particular liking for shallow water that is well aerated by surf or strong tides. Brackish water also has a special attraction for them, and for this reason they are frequently found in river estuaries, and sometimes far upstream almost to the limits of the tides. Normally, however, those fish found a long way up-river are rather small.

Feeding Habits: Sandeels, sprats, whitebait, prawns, lugworms and shore crabs all help to satisfy the bass's voracious appetite. This fish is a vigorous hunter, never remaining long in one place. Along a surf-pounded beach it will venture right into the white water, in search of sea-bed creatures exposed by the back-scour.

Small bass are always found in schools, but the adult fish are individualists, often roaming alone or with just a few companions. These solitary fish will, however, 'gang up' against a shoal of sprats, whitebait or other small fry, and the angler can sometimes locate these concentrations of bass by the slicks of sprat or whitebait oil which float to the surface, or by the seabirds attracted to the scene of the massacre.

Complete Guide to Sea Fishing

Shore Fishing Methods: (i) Surf fishing from the beach, using an inconspicuous nylon monofilament paternoster or leger. The size of hook varies according to the type of bait used, but a selection ranging from 3 to 4/0 will meet most requirements. (ii) Float fishing from rocks, pier or jetty. (iii) Spinning from a suitable rock or jetty—or from an estuary sand-spit bordering the main channel. (iv) Driftlining from the end of a jetty or pier. (v) Ground fishing with a monofilament leger or paternoster from a suitable estuary shore.

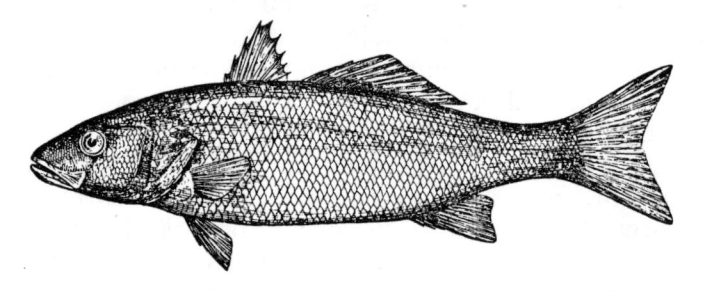

Boat Fishing Methods: (i) Driftlining in a fair run of tide, using a long flowing trace and automatic release lead. (ii) Legering in an estuary tideway when the bass are feeding on the bottom, using peeler crab bait. (iii) Trolling in or near an estuary, paying special attention to tide-washed sand-bars and rocks. Also around a rocky headland, or steep-to rocky islets. (iv) Spinning from a drifting boat. (v) Float fishing in a shallow rocky cove or inlet.

Baits: Sandeels (alive if possible), live prawns (bunched, if small), large ragworm, lugworm, peeler and soft crabs (best when fished on the bottom), squid or cuttlefish tentacles and cuttings, strips of mackerel, herring or pilchard, skate liver (boat and jetty fishing), sprats, small rock-pool eels (threaded on a long-shanked hook), razorfish, kipper, bloater.

General Observations: One of the most fascinating things about bass is the way their habits vary from one stretch of coast to another. In one estuary they may look at nothing but sandeels, while in another—sometimes less than ten

Sea Fish A. B. C.

miles away—this same bait will be ignored completely, although peeler crab or prawns will be accepted readily enough.

Even more variable are the numbers of bass caught from district to district.

A reasonably competent angler, fishing a good bass estuary, does not regard a dozen fish taken in a single trip as an outstanding bag. Yet many other rodmen, fishing regularly and just as expertly from open beaches far from any freshwater outflow, would be overjoyed to catch a dozen fair-sized bass during the course of a whole year.

The dinghy angler who drifts quietly at night in a small cove, and allows a large live prawn to swim close in to the rocks, will often make contact with some good bass. Such places are usually shallow and almost tideless, so no lead need be used. Sometimes a quiet pull on the oars every few seconds helps matters along, but on a very quiet night it may be better just to drift, and use a small partly-filled bubble float that is only just buoyant enough to break the surface.

Shore fishing in such places is usually very difficult, owing to the rocky nature of the bottom. If it can be managed however, results will often be far better than on an open stretch of beach. One way to reduce the risk of snagged tackle is to use the 'sandbag sinker', described in Chapter 3.

Although various trolling techniques have already been described in this book, we have not so far mentioned a very specialised method of power trolling for bass near tide-swept shoals.

This method of fishing originated, I am told, at Felixstowe. Here there is a stretch of shoals over the which the tide runs very strongly, and it is often impossible to use the ordinary 'back-and-forth' trolling methods carried on over less dangerous shoals and sand-bars. Instead, the boat has to be worked along the up-tide edge of the shoal, so that the bait streams right across the shallows to the down-tide edge where the bass are to be found.

Owing to the strength of the tide, it is necessary to keep

the boat facing dead into the current—or very nearly so.

A narrow gap in the shoal is usually a profitable place, and when fishing opposite one the boat is made to 'hover' almost motionless in the current. (See Fig. 31).

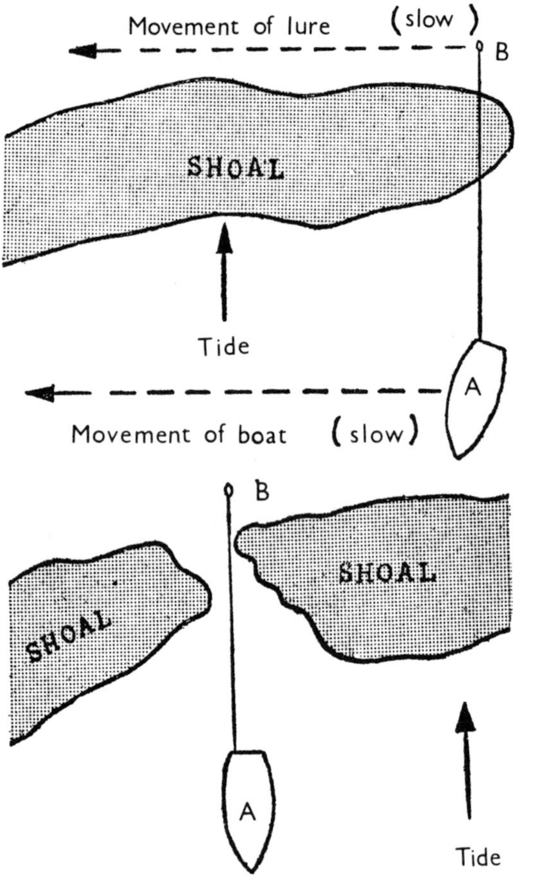

Figs. 30 and 31.   Trolling over tide-swept shoals.

Alternatively, when ranging along the edge of the shoal, the boat is allowed to run off at a very slight angle to the current, so that it moves 'crabwise' very slowly. (See Fig. 30).

Sea Fish A. B. C.

Obviously there is an element of danger in fishing under such conditions, and it is necessary to be very confident of one's engine before attempting it. However, although I do not recommend any inexperienced boat angler to try this method under such hazardous conditions, it is worth emphasising that there are many other less dangerous shoals around the coast where it could be practised without risk. Needless to say, one must always go about it intelligently, with due regard to the weather, sea conditions and depth of water over the shoals.

One great advantage of this method is that there is no propeller disturbance near the fish. The lure is worked a considerable distance from the boat, and does not follow in its wake, but takes a parallel course.

° BLACK BREAM

The so-called black bream is not really black. Coloration is variable, but the majority are a dark bluish-grey on the back, shading to silvery-grey lower down. British rod-caught record: 6 lb. 1 oz. (Skerries, 1969).

Location and Season: Black bream are somewhat limited in their distribution. Round about May they begin to appear off the coasts of Sussex, parts of the Isle of Wight, and along the Hampshire coast east of Spithead. In June they begin to show up off Dorset, South Devon and the Channel Islands. They remain until early autumn.

Haunts: The fish are usually found deep down over areas of weedy rock. In some places black bream can be caught from the beach or pier, but these fish are usually—but not invariably—rather small. From deep marks it is not unusual to take fish weighing up to 3 lb. or more.

Feeding Habits: Diet includes small sea-bed creatures such as shrimps, small molluscs and worms. Also reputed to feed to some extent on seaweed.

Shore Fishing Methods: (i) Light nylon monofilament paternoster or leger, cast out from a beach bordering a weed-bed. (ii) Deep driftlining or sliding float tackle from the end of a pier or jetty—preferably one with wooden, weed-grown piles.

Boat Fishing Methods: The black bream is a very sporting proposition on a light and lively rod, and a driftline carrying a size 6 or 8 hook on a fine monofilament trace about 2 yards in length.

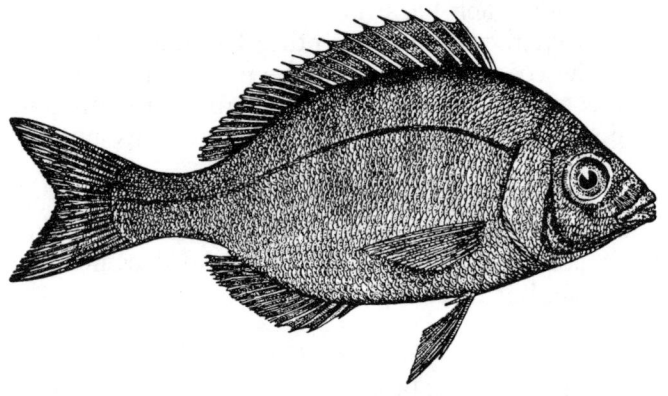

An alternative arrangement is to attach a trace of similar length above the lead, thus making a kind of single-hook paternoster. In this way it is possible to feel the lead bump on the bottom before the hook has a chance to get caught up in rocks or weed.

About 4 ft. off the bottom is usually the right fishing depth for a fairly deep mark, but don't be afraid to experiment if the fish are slow to bite. Slow reeling in for a few feet very often improves results.

Ground-baiting with crushed crabs and fish entrails, lowered in a weighted net bag, also helps to bring the fish on the feed when they are shy.

Baits: Lugworm, ragworm, mussels, mackerel and herring strips.

RED BREAM

This species of sea bream is bright crimson on the back, shading to silvery-red underneath. Adult fish have a dark patch on either side, near the commencement of the lateral line, but these 'thumb-marks' are not present on immature fish. Small red bream lacking these marks are often referred to as chad. British rod-caught record: 7 lb. 8 oz. (Fowey, 1925).

Location and Season: Encountered throughout the summer months, mainly around the coasts of south-east England and Wales, the English Channel, and western and southern Ireland.

Haunts: Areas of weedy rock. The fish are usually found near the bottom, but sometimes they may be contacted at higher levels.

Shore Fishing Methods: Red bream caught from the shore are usually rather small 'chad'. In the West Country they are commonly taken with driftline or sliding float tackle fished deep from a suitable harbour wall, jetty or steep-to rock. Evening or early morning are the best times.

Boat Fishing Methods: Similar to those used for Black Bream. Inshore fishing is best on a quiet evening. It pays to use fine tackle when the water is clear.

Baits: Mussel, ragworm, lugworm, slips of mackerel or pilchard, shrimps, limpet. Fairly small baits, with hooks to match, are usually best. Do not leave too much of the bait dangling from the hook; otherwise the bream may succeed in taking the bait without being caught.

BRILL

This flatfish is somewhat similar in appearance to the turbot, but the body is more oval, it is covered with small scales, and there are no bony tubercles. The fish is mottled and speckled brown above, and white underneath.

Fishing methods and baits are similar to those recommended for turbot. Although brill are caught mainly by the boat angler, they are sometimes taken from the shore or pier-head in a few areas.

British rod-caught record: 16 lb. (Derby Haven, Isle of Man, 1950).

° COALFISH
(Also known in Scotland as *Saithe*)

The coalfish closely resembles the pollack, but is usually darker in colour—bluish-black above, and silvery underneath. It may be distinguished by the straight white lateral line. This is curved and dark in the pollack. The lower jaw of the coalfish is only slightly longer than its upper jaw; whereas the pollack's is considerably longer. Young coalfish are commonly referred to as billet or cuddies.

British rod-caught record: 30 lb. 12 oz. (Eddystone, 1973).

Location and Season: Encountered mainly around Scotland and the northern halves of England and Ireland, but also present over deep-water reefs and wrecks off southwestern coasts—particularly in winter.

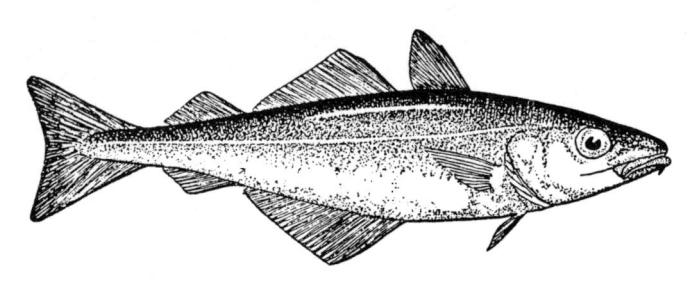

Haunts: Coalfish are usually found over reefs, in the vicinity of rugged headlands, and in rocky sounds and sealochs. Normally they swim close to the bottom, but often hunt at other levels, and at such times they may rove far from their normal rocky haunts. Also, they tend to rise towards the surface around dawn and in the evening.

Feeding Habits: Billet have a varied diet which includes marine worms, shrimps, sandeels, whitebait and other

Fig. 32. Cuddy fly.

Sea Fish A. B. C.

small fry. Adult coalfish feed mainly on other fish, such as herring and sprats.

Shore Fishing Methods: (i) Sliding float tackle from rocks, harbour wall or jetty. (ii) Spinning from rocks, harbour wall or jetty, using a small silver spoon, small 'Red Gill' sandeel or (at dusk), a fluorescent plastic eel. (iii) Working a single cuddy fly bound with shiny tinsel or 'Lurex' thread.

Boat Fishing Methods: As recommended for pollack.

Baits: Ragworm (billet), herring strip or sprat (coalfish).

° COD

This fish is so familiar a sight on the fishmonger's slab that a lengthy description is hardly necessary. The colour of its body varies, but is usually brownish, greenish or olive-grey—frequently, but not invariably, mottled or spotted. The mouth is large and the upper jaw is longer than the lower one. A barbule hangs from the lower jaw.

At the time of writing the British rod-caught record for cod stands at 32 lb. (Lowestoft Pier, 1945), but the angler can regard any cod over 10 lb. as a very good fish, and the great majority will be considerably smaller. Those under 6 lb. are usually referred to as codling.

Location and Season: Although cod may be taken throughout the winter months almost anywhere in British waters, it is around the northern and eastern coasts that the best sport is obtained. In the south, as a general rule, these fish are few and far between; although in certain seasons they are taken in good numbers towards the eastern end of the Channel.

Haunts: Cod are roving fish, and are usually encountered in shoals close to the bottom. They often favour sandy or 'scrubby' ground (weedy rocks scattered thickly over sand or muddy sand), but are liable to wander wherever food is plentiful.

Feeding Habits: Very varied. Diet includes smaller fish, small crabs, shrimps, prawns, cuttlefish, squid, marine worms, etc.

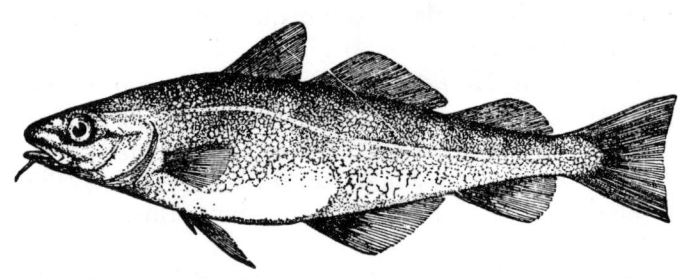

Shore Fishing Methods: Leger or paternoster tackle from pier or steeply shelving beach. Also casting out from a steep-to rock on to a snag-free patch of sea-bed.
Boat Fishing Methods: (i) Paternoster or paternoster-trot. (ii) a driftline fished just above the bottom. (iii) Working a feathered trace from a drifting boat.
Baits: Mussel, lugworm, large herring cuttings, sprats, peeler, crab, squid. Don't be afraid to use a large hook and bait—the cod has a big mouth, and an appetite to match it!

° CONGER

The conger is not everybody's fish. With its serpent-like head, baleful eyes and long, slimy body, this large sea eel is certainly an ugly customer. Yet looks are not everything, and a large and powerful conger is capable of putting up a formidable fight in its own rather disconcerting 'no holds barred' fashion.

At the time of writing the British rod-caught record stands at 96 lb. 4 oz. (off Berry Head, 1973), but there are conger swimming in the sea which would turn the scales at almost double this figure. To prove this, enormous conger are occasionally washed up dead on our beaches— one well-authenticated example being the specimen of approximately 150 lb. which was found on a Norfolk beach in 1956.

Haunts: Rocky areas of sea-bed, sunken wrecks, underwater caverns, etc.
Feeding Habits: Diet includes pouting, wrasse, **pollack,** poor cod, squid and various kinds of small rock fish. The conger is mainly a nocturnal feeder, and after sundown

it often roams fairly extensively over neighbouring areas of sand, gravel or mud. In the perpetual gloom of deep water, however, conger also hunt by day when the tides are favourable.

Shore Fishing: There is a certain stage in the conger's life-cycle when its body begins rapidly to grow thicker in relation to its length, and it is only then that the average eel begins to display signs of its future fighting qualities. It is impossible to lay down hard and fast rules, but generally few conger under about 10 lb. are capable of providing interesting sport—they just haven't got the bulk and weight.

Of course, this does not mean that smaller ones give themselves up without a struggle. They have a genius for creating difficulties, and even a puny 'whipjack' may break you if it manages to lap its tail about a rock.

One's chances of taking large conger when shore fishing depend very much upon local conditions. Plenty weighing 40 lb. and upwards live close inshore along rugged coasts where there are underwater caverns, large rock crevices and other suitable hide-outs.

Some surprisingly large conger are also found in almost rockless estuaries, where old wooden jetties, eroded stone quays, or sunken hulks provide them with shelter. Indeed, one of the biggest conger I have ever caught had its lair in a rusty ship's boiler, which lay in only a fathom of water at low Springs, in an almost entirely sandy Scottish firth.

Although conger may be hooked occasionally when daylight beach fishing, the ideal time to start tackling up is at the first signs of dusk, preferably on a calm evening in summer or autumn. If there is a hint of thunder in the air, so much the better.

Most fresh or frozen fish baits will arouse a conger's interest, but when you are trying to attract a big one from its normal hunting grounds some distance beyond casting range there's nothing to beat an oily bait, such as herring or mackerel. Squid and freshly caught pouting are also excellent.

The bait should normally be presented on or near the sea-bed. The type of tackle most generally favoured is a free-running leger carrying a swivelled trace that cannot be bitten through by the conger's sharp and powerful teeth. Wire is often used, but a length of soft 'unbiteable' commercial trot-line snooding often makes for easier shore casting.

Also, it is interesting to note that wire traces are distrusted by some conger specialists who habitually fish from shingle beaches. Their theory is that the eels, dragging at the bait, are put off by the vibrations caused when the wire moves over the pebbly bottom.

The conger's habit of dragging cautiously at the bait before finally accepting it is the main reason for choosing a running leger. With this type of tackle, of course, line can be yielded without the eel feeling any resistance from the lead.

It is most important not be in too great a hurry to strike when a conger mouths the bait. Usually you will feel the line inching away slowly for a few seconds; then comes a pause—after which the line begins to glide away again. This is your signal to drive the hook home.

If you've hooked a big one—and you won't be left long in doubt on this score!—you must do everything possible to keep it away from rocks, jetty piles or other obstructions. Adopt the tactics of a policeman arresting a tough character. Don't stop to argue—just keep the eel on the move until it is safely in custody!

Sea Fish A. B. C.

Normally, before shore angling with leger tackle you will have to find a place close to a suitable rocky area where it is possible to cast out to a patch of reasonably snag-free ground. However, if the sea-bed is too rough for an ordinary lead, you may be able to use a sandbag sinker, paternoster fashion, below a one-hook swivelled trace.

Where a snag-free sea-bed comes right up close to the base of longshore rocks, it may be possible to use one of the rocks as a fishing stance. In this event, try casting the bait in the vicinity of a suspected conger lair—but don't place it *too* close to the rocks. Otherwise the eel will drag it into the nearest crevice before you are ready to strike.

This advice also holds good when fishing from old sea-eroded harbour breakwaters, lifeboat slipways, piers and other likely conger spots.

Landing a really big conger from such places may be fraught with difficulties, however, and it is wise to give this problem some thought before starting to fish. No matter how promising an angling spot may seem, there is little point in using it if, on hooking the longed-for monster, you cannot get a gaff within yards of it.

After successfully capturing even a medium-sized conger, treat its powerful, sharp-toothed jaws with respect. Don't attempt to remove the hook; instead, unclip it from the swivel-link attachment and fit another.

Remember, too, that it is your responsibility to see that the eel does not bite off the finger of some over-inquisitive child, or the nose of a sniffing dog. Both these things have happened more than once, and the safest place for a conger is inside a strong and securely tied sack.

Boat Fishing: The boat angler in search of a *big* conger will do best to try for them near a sunken wreck, or among sea-bed rocks which are full of cavern-like splits and crevices, or which have become undercut by the erosion of strong tides.

Large and snaggy upthrusts like these make it all too easy for the angler to lose his tackle, while at the same time giving the conger plenty of opportunities to lap its tremendously powerful tail round an obstruction. However, there are various tactics which can help to prevent this sort of thing happening.

The most common one is to anchor the boat up-tide of the mark. Strong leger tackle is then weighted so that it slants down on the tide, and comes to rest on the sea-bed about 10 yards or so from the edge of the rocks.

The slant of the line should suit the nature of the sea-bed. When the ground around the mark is reasonably clear of obstructions, the line can be sent down at an angle of about 45 degrees. When there are some outlying snags, however, the line will have to be weighted so that it sinks much more steeply.

It is important not to place the tackle too close to the rocks, because most conger will pull the bait gently back towards the rocks before they finally accept it. A delayed strike is necessary, as described under Shore Fishing.

Usually the battle is won or lost in the first second or two after striking.

The main thing is to pile on pressure immediately, and get the conger away from the rocks or wreck. For obvious reasons, therefore, it is advisable to use a non-stretch type of line, such as braided terylene.

A really good conger mark, which will be fished time and time again, is worth surveying carefully. A pretty clear picture of its extent can be obtained by making several runs across the mark with the echo-sounder working; or, if you lack this modern aid, by dragging a heavy weight along the sea-bed.

The actual positioning of the boat must be done carefully, heading slowly into the tide for the desired distance after the echo-sounder, or the feel of the bumping lead, denotes a change from rocky bottom to soft ground.

Provided that care is taken with these preliminaries, and there is no cross-wind to make the boat yaw at its anchor, fairly accurate positioning should be possible in a reasonable depth of water.

There are occasions, of course, when the sea-bed surrounding a particularly rewarding conger mark is too

Sea Fish A. B. C.

broken up with other rocks to allow the bait to be legered on the bottom. Under such conditions it is necessary to entice the conger to a bait suspended above the rocks. Your best chance of doing this will be at night, but it is a good plan to go out in the evening while there is still sufficient daylight to take up position accurately over the mark. Calm and rather sultry conditions usually provide good sport.

For this 'above the rocks' method of conger fishing it is possible to use the tackle illustrated in Fig. 33. The trace (not shown) is attached to the spiral locking clip (A), and a streamlined lead suspended on about 1 ft. of line (B), so that the bump of the lead on the rocky bottom will act as a warning before the hook has a chance to become snagged.

This lead line, incidentally, should be weaker than the rest of the tackle, so that only the lead will be lost if it becomes caught up on the bottom.

The amount of lead should be chosen with care. It should be heavy enough to take the line down fairly close to the vertical, because if the line slants too much on the tide it will allow the conger to swim downwards in an arc, like the weight on a pendulum, and so gain the safety of the rocks.

On the other hand, the lead must not be heavier than is absolutely necessary, otherwise it will cause too much drag when the conger samples the bait.

When fishing a mark where real monsters are likely to be encountered, it is best to use a swivelled trace of plastic-covered cable-laid wire. This type of trace is flexible, and streams out quite nicely in a good run of tide; especially when it is carrying a fillet of mackerel, herring, or some other large fish bait.

However, conger tackle can be lost very easily among sea-bed snags, and many anglers will have to economise by using a cheaper kind of trace. Stiff single-strand wire is not recommended, but it is possible to obtain good results with a swivelled trace of very strong nylon monofilament—say 80 lb. breaking strain.

At the end of this trace a strong and very sharp hook is attached by means of a stainless spiral locking clip and about eight inches of 50 to 80 lb. breaking strain cable-laid stainless wire.

The importance of having really efficient swivels cannot be overemphasised, because a hooked conger will often whirl round and round like a top. Two or three swivels will be sufficient, but they must be robustly made of solid brass or stainless steel.

We have already mentioned that conger are cautious biters. Sometimes, though, when using this tackle above the rocks, an interested conger can be coaxed into making a more determined grab at the bait by slowly reeling it up a few feet.

Some chopped-up pilchards, mackerel or herring, placed in a net-bag and attached about two fathoms up the anchor rope, will send an attractive scent streaming over the tops of the rocks, and make the conger more willing to swim upwards. The bag should be made of strong, close-meshed netting, in case a conger decides to test its teeth on it.

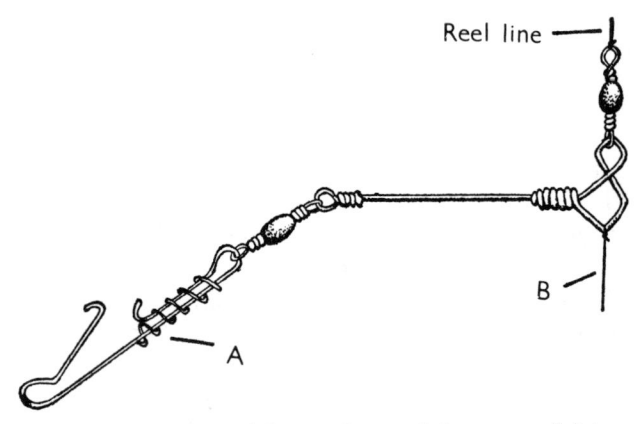

Fig. 33. Tackle for 'above the rocks' conger fishing.

Yet another way to get conger in a feeding mood, when the water is shallow and the current not too swift, is to throw a few chunks of fish bait into the water. In deeper

Sea Fish A. B. C.

water, of course, this groundbait would be carried too far away by the tide to be of any use. To overcome this problem, however, it is possible to use an enlarged version of the automatic swim-feeders used by freshwater anglers.

DAB

The Common Dab is one of our smallest flatfish. Its body is a lightish sandy colour on the back, with or without darker spots, and white underneath. The lateral line curves upwards abruptly above the pectoral fin, and the scales on the white underside are smooth. British rod-caught record: 2 lb. 10 oz. 12 dr. (The Skerries, 1968).

The Long Rough Dab is brownish above, without spots, and white below. The lateral line has only a slight curve above the pectoral fin, and the scales towards the posterior end of the white underside are rough.

Location and Season: The common dab is the species most frequently caught by anglers, and it may be encountered all round the British Isles throughout most of the year. It is during the summer, autumn and early winter, however, that these fish are most likely to be found close inshore.

Haunts: Lives on the bottom in areas of sand or sandy mud. Often common in shallow bays.

Feeding Habits: Diet includes lugworms, razorfish, hermit crabs, starfish and many other small sea-bed creatures.

Shore Fishing Methods: Casting out on to sand from a pier or beach, using a light monofilament paternoster or paternoster-trot. Use small, fine-wire, long-shanked hooks.

Boat Fishing Methods: Tackle as for shore fishing.

Baits: Lugworm, ragworm, mussel, razorfish, hermit crab tails.

DOGFISH, LESSER SPOTTED

This is the smaller of the two species of spotted dogfish, and is not a very interesting proposition from the point of view of sport. It has a very rough skin, which is mostly sandy coloured and 'peppered' with numerous small dark spots. The underside is white. This fish may be distinguished from the Greater Spotted Dogfish (q.v.) by the nasal flaps—those of the Lesser Spotted possess a simple curved edge, whilst those of the Greater Spotted are lobed.

Location and Season: Found all round the British Isles at most seasons of the year.
Haunts: Usually found close to the bottom, in sandy or muddy areas.
Feeding Habits: Feeds largely on crabs of various kinds. starfish, and other sea-bed creatures. It is fond of fish, however, and will rob nets and longlines.
Shore Fishing Methods: Rarely fished for deliberately, but is frequently taken when legering or paternostering from pier or beach.
Boat Fishing Methods: Frequently taken when ground fishing on sand or mud.
Baits: Strips of mackerel, herring or pilchard, sprat 'cutlets'.

DOGFISH, GREATER SPOTTED

Also known as the Bull Huss, this fish closely resembles the Lesser Spotted Dogfish (q.v.). It attains a larger size, however, and the general coloration of the body is darker, and the spots are larger. It is not a sporting species, but makes quite good eating after it has been skinned. British rod-caught record: 21 lb. 3 oz. (Looe, 1955).
Location and Season: Found all round the British Isles at most seasons, but is most numerous in the south.
Haunts: Rocky and 'scrubby' ground.
Feeding Habits: Feeds mostly near the bottom on crabs, small lobsters, and slow-swimming species of bottom fish.

DOGFISH, SPUR

Puts up a somewhat better fight than the two species of dogfish previously mentioned. Its body is usually dark grey or brown above, with a few whitish spots. The underside is white. Perhaps the most noteworthy feature, however, are the 'spurs'—one in front of each dorsal fin. These are capable of causing a nasty wound, which very often turns septic—so handle the fish with care, preferably pinning it down and nipping off the spurs with a pair of long-nosed pliers. British Record: 20 lb. 3 oz. (Needles, 1972).
Location and Season: Found all round the British Isles, and

Sea Fish A.B.C.

is most likely to be encountered by inshore anglers during the summer months.

Haunts: Nomadic.

Feeding Habits: Preys on other fish, and robs nets and long-lines.

Fishing Methods: Usually caught when fishing for other species, and may be encountered at any level.

Baits: Lugworm, mussel, and strips of herring, mackerel, pilchard, whiting, etc.

° FLOUNDER

This flatfish cannot truthfully be called a sporting species, but fishing for it can be pleasant and interesting on light tackle. The colour of its upper side is usually dark brown or almost black, and below it is a brilliant opaque white. Not infrequently there are faint mottled markings, or lighter patches, on the coloured side. British rod-caught record: 5 lb. 11 oz. 8 dr. (Fowey, 1956).

Location and Season: Found all round the British Isles, and is most likely to be caught on rod and line in summer, autumn and winter.

Haunts: During the seasons mentioned above, flounders are common in estuaries and tidal reaches of rivers where the bottom is mud, muddy sand, or sand. In late winter and spring the adult fish move out into the open sea to spawn.

Feeding Habits: Like other flatfish, the flounder spends most of its time on or near the bottom. Nevertheless, it is an active hunter, and in many areas sandeels, whitebait and similar small fish form quite an important part of its diet. For the most part, however, adult flounders feed on lug and various other marine worms, sand shrimps, small shore crabs, etc.

Shore Fishing Methods: Shore fishing for flounders can be carried on from a variety of vantage points, including pier, jetty, harbour wall, open sandy or muddy beaches, moored barges, or an estuary shore that provides firm footing within casting distance of a fairly deep channel.

During the flood tide, especially on warm sunny days, flounders swim in over shallow mud and sandflats. But as the tide ebbs they retire once more to the deeper channels, and at such times, their numbers being more concentrated, it is often easier for the angler to make contact with them.

Flounders like a fair amount of water movement, and for this reason they are more likely to be found in the main channels than in creeks and subsidiary channels which, although fairly deep, meander out of the main flow of tide.

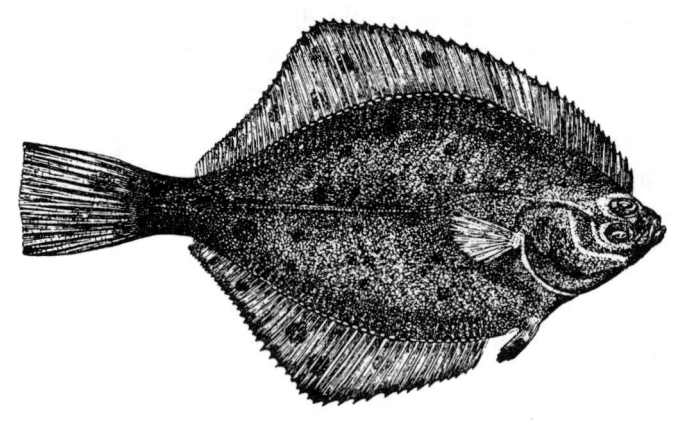

Light tackle is naturally best for this modest-sized flattie, but don't lose sight of the fact that in many estuaries the bait may also be taken by hard-fighting bass. Suitable traces include a one or two-hook monofilament leger, or a two-hook paternoster-trot.

From a jetty, steep-to embankment or other suitable vantage point, it is sometimes possible to spin with a baited flounder spoon. A plastic spoon usually gives good results, especially when coloured on one side, and white on the other.

However, it is important to use the correct type of spoon, which should be designed so that only the spoon revolves—not the bait. Also it should be fitted with a long-shanked, fine wire hook—not a treble. A small additional hook may also be mounted higher up to hold the head of

Sea Fish A. B. C.

the worm, and prevent it sliding back down the shank of the main hook.

Boat Fishing Methods: When fishing from a boat the tackle is often streamed down-tide until it touches bottom, and there it is allowed to rest until a fish—or crabs!—take the bait. However, flounders are attracted by a moving bait, and whether fishing from shore or boat, repeated casting out and reeling in often helps to produce bites.

Provided that the bed of the channel is not fouled by rocks, weed or moorings, the dinghy angler can save himself the bother of casting by drag-lining with the tide. In some estuaries the best time for this is about an hour before to about an hour after slack water, when the run of tide is not too swift.

If the bottom is foul, or crabs are a nuisance, then either light float tackle can be fished deep, or a baited spoon trolled slowly with oars. The spoon is similar to that recommended for shore fishing, but can be rather larger—say 3 in. It should be trolled with the tide.

Baits: Ground fishing and drag-lining—lugworm, ragworm. Float fishing—ragworm, live shrimp. Baited spoon—ragworm, lugworm. In addition, at certain seasons and places (usually near estuary sand-flats) live sandeels can be very killing. Peeler and soft crabs vary widely in their appeal, but are sometimes useful for ground fishing.

GARFISH

This strange-looking fish has a bluish-silver eel-like body, and a long beaked mouth. It is known by a variety of local names, such as Longnose, Needlefish and Spearfish. On light tackle it can provide good sport, very often leaping right out of the water—and sometimes even turning cartwheels on the surface!

Location and Season: A summer visitor to most British coasts, and is frequently encountered in areas where mackerel are abundant.

Haunts: Nomadic.

Feeding Habits: Preys on whitebait, sandeels and other small fry.

Fishing Methods: Can be taken by most of the shore and boat methods recommended for mackerel. The main difficulty is to make the hook lodge firmly in the garfish's beaked mouth. It often helps if the strike is delayed for a second or two until the fish is heading away from the angler; the hook will then be pulled back into the corner of the mouth. For the same reason a sideways strike is usually better than an upwards one. The garfish's beak can quickly damage a monofilament hook link, so inspect your terminal tackle after every catch.
Baits: Mackerel strips, whole whitebait, small sandeels or small silvery-coloured trolling and spinning lures.

GURNARDS

Six species of gurnard are found around the coasts of Britain, but not all are of interest to the angler. The Red Gurnard, Tub and Piper are reddish in colour, but the Grey Gurnard (one of the commonest species) is usually slate-grey on the back and sides, with or without white markings, and white underneath. British rod-caught record (Tub): 11 lb. 7 oz. 4 dr. (Wallasey, 1952).
Location and Season: Found around the coasts of England, Wales and Ireland, the distribution range varying with the species. Most common inshore during the summer months.
Haunts: Mostly found on sandy areas of sea-bed, or near rocks which are bordered by sand.
Feeding Habits: Diet includes various kinds of shrimps, small crabs, marine worms, small fish, etc.
Shore Fishing: Not fished for deliberately on most coasts, but in suitable areas gurnard are sometimes taken on a baited spoon worked close to the sea-bed.
Boat Fishing: Not often fished for deliberately, but sometimes taken when legering with light tackle. Alter-

Sea Fish A.B.C.

natively, can be caught by trolling a baited spoon just above the sea-bed.
Baits: Ragworm, mackerel strip, shrimp, small sandeel.

HADDOCK

This member of the cod family is greyish-bronze on the back, shading to white underneath. The lateral line is black, and there is a black blotch or 'thumb-mark' above each pectoral fin. Record: 10 lb. 12 oz. (Looe, 1972).
Location and Season: The haddock was once common on many British coasts, but its numbers have been drastically reduced by over-fishing. The majority of fish nowadays are taken around the coasts of Scotland, north-east England, Northern Ireland, and the northern North Sea. They come fairly close inshore during the winter.
Feeding Habits: Swims over soft areas of sea-bed, feeding on various kinds of shrimps, crabs, starfish, etc.
Fishing Methods: Haddock are normally caught when boat fishing, and either leger or paternoster tackle can be used. The fish move all the time as they feed, so drifting tactics may increase the chance of contacting a shoal.
Baits: Mussel is probably best, but soft crab, bunched lugworm and ragworm, and strips of herring, mackerel and pilchard are also useful. Mussel tipped with squid tentacle is also reputed to be very good.

HAKE

Another member of the cod family that has become scarce as a result of over-fishing. Body long and slender; grey above, and silvery-white along the sides and belly. Large mouth with long, sharp teeth. British rod-caught record: 25 lb. 5 oz. 8 dr. (Belfast Lough, 1962).
Location and Season: A deep-water fish which is most likely to be encountered off the coasts of Cornwall, southern and western Ireland, and western and northern Scotland. Normally caught on rod and line in summer and autumn—but nowadays this is not very often.
Fishing Methods: Rarely fished for deliberately, but occasionally takes a whole mackerel or similar fish bait

placed on the bottom for conger. The hake's sharp teeth make it advisable to use wire next to the hook.

HALIBUT

A giant flatfish which, in Scottish waters, has been caught on rod and line to a weight of 161 lb. 12 oz. (Orkney, 1968). The upper side of its body is a dark olive colour, marbled with lighter markings, and white underneath.

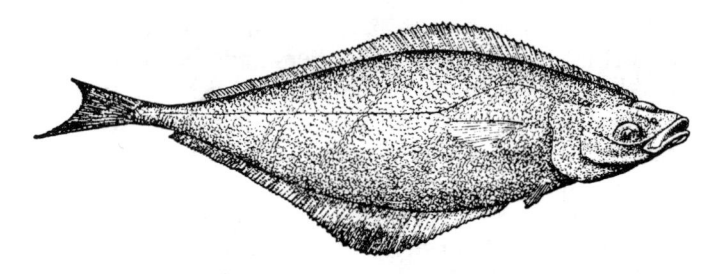

Location: A cold-water fish, and in British waters is found mostly off northernmost Scotland, notably around the Pentland Firth and Orkney. It is a powerful and active feeder.

Fishing Methods: Drift-fishing with fish baits (whiting, small haddock, coalfish or mackerel), presented just above the bottom. Tackle as recommended for giant skate.

HERRING

The herring is so familiar that it requires no description. It feeds mainly on plankton, and for this reason anglers believed for many years that it could not be caught on a baited hook.

Nowadays, however, herring are taken in considerable numbers in some areas by anglers using light quill float gear, and baiting size 10 hooks with tiny harbour ragworm. The fishing is done on winter nights, in places where quayside or embankment lights attract herring into deep-water harbours or estuaries. Three hooks are used as a rule, spaced out on a trace about 5—6 ft. long—two hooks being on 3 in. monofilament droppers, and the bottom hook suspended from the end of the trace.

Sea Fish A.B.C.

Herring can also be caught by working a trace of tiny feathered hooks from a boat.

JOHN DORY

This is one of the queerest-looking fish found in British waters, for its huge mouth is folded in concertina fashion, enabling it to be extended forwards suddenly for several inches.

A fish-eater, the John Dory is too slow and ungainly to catch its prey by normal methods. Instead, this clownish-looking creature swims slowly and innocently towards its intended victim, and when close enough suddenly shoots its mouth across the intervening gap!

The John Dory is common around West Country coasts, and western and southern Ireland. In these areas it is frequently taken by anglers using live fish baits—especially sandeels. British rod-caught record: 10 lb. 12 oz. (Porthallow, Cornwall, 1963).

LING

This long and rather slimy fish is usually greenish or brownish grey on the back, becoming lighter below. A barbule hangs from its lower jaw. The fish attains a considerable size, and those caught by commercial fishermen occasionally weigh over 50 lb. British rod-caught record: 45 lb. (Penzance, 1912).

Location: Found all round the British Isles.
Haunts: A deep-water species, it normally swims close to the bottom, favouring rocky areas.
Feeding Habits: Preys on other fish.
Fishing Methods: Sizable ling are nearly always taken when boat fishing in fairly deep water. They can be caught on or close to the bottom, using strong leger or driftline tackle alongside a rocky mark.
Baits: Whole mackerel and similar fish baits.

° MACKEREL

With its sleek body, shimmering with greenish-blue and mother-of-pearl highlights, the mackerel is one of the most handsome fish in British waters. For its size, it is also one of the most powerful.

It is often referred to as the 'holidaymaker's fish'; for there is scarely a coastal resort in Britain where the local boatmen do not offer trips round the bay, with handlines and mackerel trolling lures supplied to those who want them. In this way, unfortunately, many inland anglers visiting the coast gain a false impression of sea fishing, and fail to appreciate the wonderful sporting possibilities of this fish.

British rod-caught record: 5 lb. 6 oz. 8 dr. (N. of Eddystone Light, 1969).

Feeding Habits: With rather wide local variations, mackerel visit our inshore waters from about the middle of spring until mid-autumn, and during this period they feed largely upon whitebait and various other kinds of small fry. In pursuit of these bait shoals they roam far and fast, and often venture close inshore or enter river estuaries.

Normally mackerel are found in the upper levels of water—usually in the first 30 ft. below the surface. On occasions, however, they may go considerably deeper; while very often, when chasing shoals of whitebait, they actually break the surface. The 'rattling' of one of these mackerel sprays can be heard a long way off on a still evening, and from the crest of the beach the disturbed water is visible for a couple of miles or more. Sometimes it will appear as a dark patch, like a catspaw; sometimes as a sudden burst of white foam which vanishes as abruptly as it appeared.

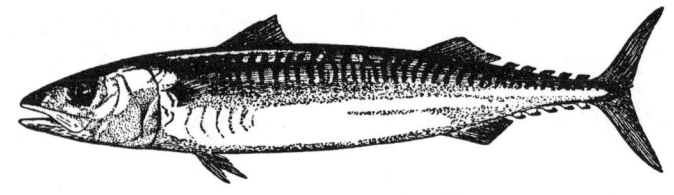

Shore Fishing Methods: Mackerel seldom remain long in one place, and success depends very largely upon making

Sea Fish A.B.C.

the most of one's opportunities when a shoal comes within range.

From rocks, harbour wall or pier, light float tackle is often used, with a cutting of fresh-caught mackerel or garfish on a size 2 hook.

Spinning with a threadline rod and reel from a steep-shelving beach or other suitable vantage point also provides excellent sport. Suitable artificial lures are described in Chapter 4. Alternatively, for the person compelled to use a light beachcaster with 3—4 ounces of lead, a useful terminal tackle would be a trace carrying three feathered hooks.

Boat Fishing Methods: Without a doubt, the largest catches of mackerel will be taken when using a trace of feathered lures from a drifting boat. This is the method to use when plenty of fish are needed in a hurry for bait or the frying pan, but it can hardly be called angling.

Trolling with the familiar mackerel spinner is also a killing method, and when carried on from a light pulling dinghy, as distinct from a motor boat, it is possible to obtain excellent sport with light tackle.

Float fishing for mackerel is possible from a boat, using the tackle described for shore fishing. Also, these fish are not infrequently taken when driftlining or trolling for bass, using live sandeel bait.

MONKFISH

The monkfish, otherwise known as the angel-fish, has broad, wing-like pectoral fins, and for this reason looks rather like a skate—although it is in fact a member of the shark family. The flattened head and body are brownish or greyish above, with darker and lighter blotches and spots. British rod-caught record: 66 lb. (Shoreham, 1965).

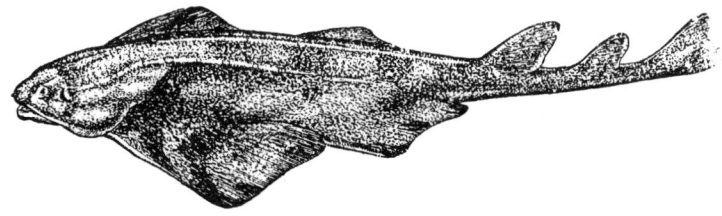

Location and Season: Most commonly caught in summer and early autumn, around the southern and western coasts of England and Ireland.
Haunts: Areas of mud, sand or mixed ground.
Feeding Habits: Preys largely upon other fish.
Fishing Methods: Usually caught by chance when ground fishing with large fish baits. Quite often taken by beach fishermen, usually at night. Certain stretches of shore appear to be visited by monkfish regularly every summer.

° MULLET, GREY

Three kinds of grey mullet are found in British waters —the Thin-Lipped, Thick-Lipped and Golden-Eyed Grey Mullet. From the angler's point of view the differences between them are slight. British rod-caught record: 10 lb. 1 oz. (Portland, 1953).
Location: May be encountered in suitable areas around most parts of the British Isles, although most numerous in the south and west.
Haunts and Seasons: Mullet have a special liking for brackish water, and are common in estuaries and creeks during the spring, summer and autumn. Mullet may also remain in estuaries during the winter in mild areas, or if there happens to be a warm water outfall from a power station in the vicinity. In the open sea, mullet are commonly encountered near rocky promontories and coves.

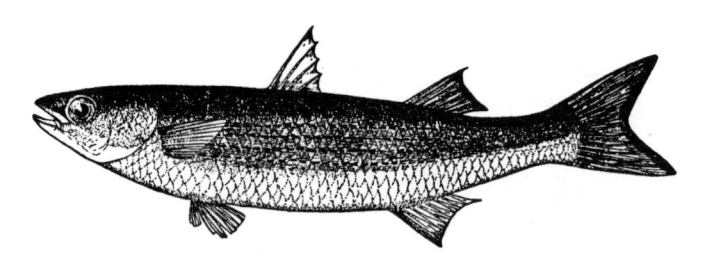

Feeding Habits: The grey mullet feeds on a mixed diet of small, soft-bodied water creatures, worms (both live and dead), and—in harbours—galley scraps thrown overboard

Sea Fish A.B.C.

from ships. They also browse upon the green silk weed growing on mooring buoys, wooden piles, stone jetties, etc

The habits of mullet may vary slightly according to local conditions, but almost everywhere, except when prevented by rough seas, the shoals follow a daily routine that is governed by the tides. Careful observation of this routine is the first step towards successful mullet fishing.

In creeks and estuaries, for instance, mullet usually work their way in with the tide, feeding as they go. Very often they follow the line of floating tidal debris, swimming at or very near the surface.

Fishing methods: Mullet are usually caught from rocks, harbour wall, pier, jetty or moored weed-grown barge or pontoon. By comparison, few are caught from boats. A very important preliminary is to groundbait the area, and many mullet specialists cast some sopped bread into the water before they start to set up their tackle. Minced pilchards, and finely chopped mackerel guts or worms are also used to attract the fish and get them feeding. Whatever type of groundbait is chosen, however, it should be used little and often.

Another important point to bear in mind is that mullet are easily scared, so it pays to make oneself as inconspicuous as possible. Above all, avoid noise or sudden movements.

Various specialised methods of mullet angling have been devised to overcome local problems, but light float fishing is the most popular and rewarding method in many areas. An Avon-type freshwater rod makes an ideal weapon for mullet fishing, and this can be used with a small-capacity fixed-spool reel loaded with 5 lb. b.s. nylon monofilament line. This may seem very light by normal sea angling standards, but mullet are suspicious of heavier, more conspicuous tackle. Depending on local conditions, you should use either a quill float or the slender cork-bodied type.

As an alternative to the Avon-type rod, you could use a light 9 or 10 ft. spinning rod.

Complete Guide to Sea Fishing

Fig. 34 shows a suitable tackle set-up. Note the extra line-holder, positioned as close to the top of the float as possible; this prevents the line below the float becoming fouled when casting.

Enough split shot should be used to take the float well down, thus reducing its resistance to fish to a minimum. The tip should be painted fluorescent red.

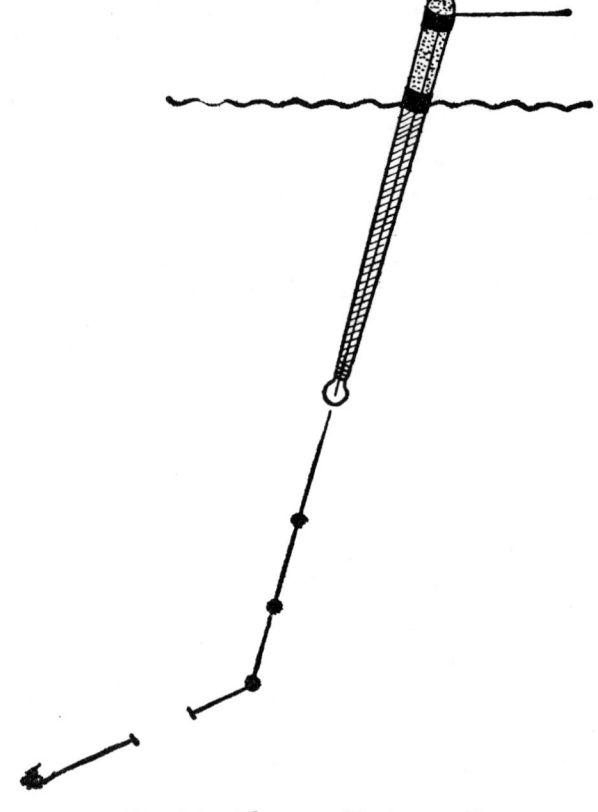

Fig. 34. Float tackle for mullet.

The bait should just cover the hook (sizes 10—14); the hook-point being needle-sharp and protruding from the bait.

Sea Fish A.B.C.

The usual float fishing techniques apply. In moving water, the float should be cast upstream and allowed to drift down, and no slack should be allowed in the line.

Strike promptly but not too vigorously, bearing in mind that the mullet has soft lips, and the hook may easily tear out if the fish is handled roughly. A landing net is essential.

Baits: Small harbour ragworm, peeled prawn and shrimp, maggots, pork or bacon fat (uncooked), fat beef (cooked), bread flake, bread crust, small portions of a peeler crab's claw or leg, skate liver, and small pieces of chopped-up mackerel or pilchard flesh.

° PLAICE

This well-known and very tasty flatfish is usually brown or greenish-brown on the back, with numerous red or orange spots, and white underneath. It is not generally regarded as a sporting species, but a decent-sized plaice will often put up quite a good fight when taken on light tackle. British rod-caught record: 7 lb. 15 oz. (Salcombe, 1964).

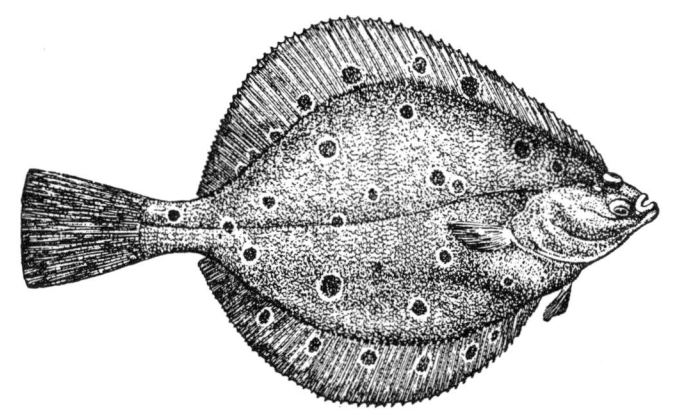

Location and Season: Found all round the British Isles, and most likely to be taken on rod and line from late spring until late autumn or early winter.

Haunts: Areas of sand, shell-grit and muddy sand.

Complete Guide to Sea Fishing

Feeding Habits: Feeds on the bottom. Diet includes burrowing molluscs, marine worms, shrimps, etc. An important point is that plaice feed readily in daylight, and unlike many other sea fish will accept a bait when the water is clear and the sun is shining brightly.

Shore Fishing Methods: Casting out a light paternoster-trot or leger on to an area of sand rich in lugworm, razorfish, etc. Use long-shanked hooks that are fine in the wire.

Boat Fishing Methods: Terminal tackle as for shore fishing. A good plaice mark, naturally enough, is one which offers plenty of suitable shell-fish food, and an abundance of broken shell mixed up with the sand on the sea-bed usually indicates these conditions.

It is also possible to discover good fishing areas by observing the activities and catches of inshore trawlers. Don't forget, though, that as a rod and line angler you have an advantage over the trawler by being able to fish plaice marks which are guarded by jagged rocks, old wrecks and suchlike snags.

Over extensive snag-free marks, drift-fishing or drag-lining also produces good results at times.

° POLLACK

The pollack closely resembles the coalfish, but it is usually lighter in colour—dark green or reddish-bronze on the back, shading through deep gold to silver on the sides and belly. The lower jaw projects considerably, and lacks the barbule carried by the coalfish. The average size varies tremendously from one coastal area to another. In some areas a 3-pounder would be considered large, but off the coasts of Cornwall and Pembrokeshire pollack of 10—15 lb. are not unusual. British rod-caught record: 25 lb. (Eddystone Light, 1972).

Location and Season: Most numerous around the north and south coasts of Cornwall, the English Channel, southwest Wales, and south and west Ireland. Most likely to be taken by the angler from late spring to mid-autumn.

Haunts: Kelpy reefs, pinnacle rocks, deepwater wrecks

Sea Fish A.B.C.

and near steep-to rocky islets. Normally found fairly close to the bottom.

Feeding Habits: Large pollack feed mainly on other fish, including sandeels, whitebait, sprats and bream. Smaller pollack also prey on fish, but their diet includes prawns, shrimps, ragworms, small swimming crabs, etc. Normally pollack seem to feed most eagerly around dawn or dusk, and at such times they sometimes rise towards the surface —especially inshore.

Shore Fishing Methods: As a rule, pollack caught from the shore are not very large, and even in Cornish waters a 5-pounder would be considered a good fish. The following methods are recommended: (i) Float fishing from a rock or harbour wall. Repeated casting and slow retrieving (float spinning) often helps to produce bites, and a favourite bait for this is ragworm, with a little of the tail trailing from the hook. (ii) Spinning with a natural fish bait, feathered squid, plastic sandeel, or (at dusk) a fluorescent plastic eel. (iii) A cuddy fly worked from a harbour wall, steep-to rock or similar vantage point. This is usually best when high water arrives around sundown. (iv) Driftlining from the end of a jetty or pier.

Boat Fishing Methods: Big pollack seem to have a special liking for the inaccessible, difficult-to-fish type of coastline, and this is one reason why their presence in some areas may have been overlooked. They are found off rugged headlands where tide-rips swirl over kelpy reefs and ledges, and overfalls roar in heavy weather.

They also favour sudden up-thrusts of submerged, crevice-riddled rock, and craggy islets which rise abruptly from a sea-bed encumbered with sea-weedy rocks.

Normally pollack swim fairly deep down, and close to the rocks. Round about dawn or dusk, however, there is a tendency for them to swim at higher levels, or even to break the surface. Weather conditions, depth of water and food requirements all combine to influence their movement.

In order to catch pollack, movement in one form or another must normally be imparted to the bait. How this is accomplished will depend very largely upon the nature of the mark.

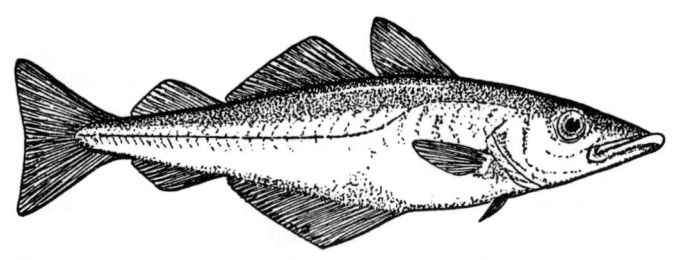

Over an extensive reef, or along a series of ledges, it is possible to use drifting or trolling tactics. In this event, dead baits or various kinds of artificials will produce satisfactory results.

On the other hand, if it is wished to fish one particularly good spot, driftlining at anchor is a rewarding method. For best results this requires a live bait, and by 'live' I also mean 'lively'—something which will swim around at the end of a light flowing trace. A sandeel is ideal, a prawn is good, and various small fish (tiny whiting, poor cod, harvest mackerel, etc.) are not to be despised.

When livebaits are unobtainable, deadbaits can be driftlined sink and draw. Send the bait right down to the depth at which the pollack are estimated to be swimming, then reel in slowly. Alternatively, it is possible to fish one or two plastic 'Red Gill' sandeels, mounted paternoster fashion on a monofilament line, so that they swim and wiggle most convincingly in the tide.

Use as long and fine a trace as practicable, so that the deadbait can work in the tide. At the same time, though, don't use a trace that is *too* long, or the pollack will be able to bore down and seek refuge among the rocks.

When driftlining, you will sometimes find that the biggest fish are the shyest biters, and a tentative pluck at the bait may well be the prelude to hooking a rod-bending monster. Don't strike at this stage. Instead, just keep reel-

Sea Fish A.B.C.

ing in slowly, and the pollack will usually make a determined grab. You will soon know then if your fish is a big one!

If it is, do everything possible to check the first tremendous downward plunge towards the sea-bed. Only occasionally have I encountered pollack which made a run, and in most cases these fish were hooked some distance away from their rocky haunts, presumably when they were pursuing shoals of whitebait.

Baits: Sandeels (preferably live), mackerel, pilchard and garfish strips, sprats and small harvest mackerel used whole, ragworm, live prawn.

POUTING

This member of the cod family has a very deep body in proportion to its length. It is mainly coppery in colour, with darker vertical bands on the sides. There is a black spot at the base of each pectoral fin, and a barbule hangs from the lower jaw. British rod-caught record: 5 lb. 8 oz. (Berry Head, 1969).

Location and Season: Although found around many parts of the British Isles, it is most numerous around south-west England and Ireland.

Haunts: Rocky and broken ground.

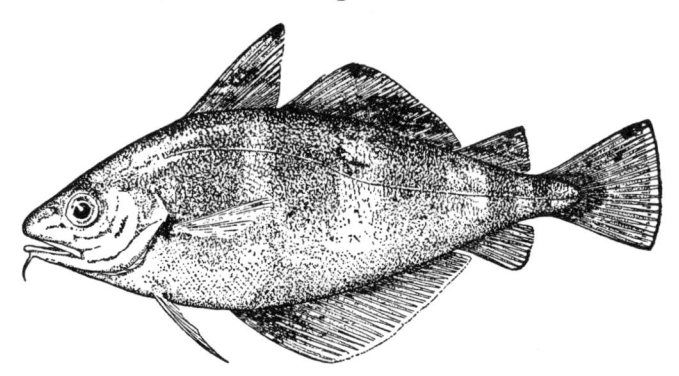

Feeding Habits: Swims near the bottom, feeding on prawns, marine worms, small shore and swimming crabs, and small rock-haunting fish.

Shore Fishing Methods: Not a very interesting fish to catch, but commonly taken from pier, harbour wall or open beach. Tackle—paternoster or leger. Fairly small hooks, say size 2, will catch the most fish, but use size 1/0 or larger if you do not wish to be pestered with the small ones.

Boat Fishing Methods: (i) Deep driftlining can give quite fair sport on light tackle in places where the pouting run to 1½ lb. or more. (ii) Paternoster fished 1—3 ft. above rough ground.

Baits: Mussels, ragworm, lugworm, mackerel and herring cuttings, shrimps, prawns, squid, shelled garden snails.

SCAD

(Also known as the *Horse Mackerel* and *Scousher*)

This fish is easily recognised by the bony plates set 'herring-bone' fashion along the lateral line. There is also a row of backward-slanting spurs on the lateral line towards the tail-end of the body. Coloration is bluish above, and silvery below the lateral line. British rod-caught record: 3 lb. 4 oz. 8 dr. (off Mewstone, Plymouth, 1971).

Location and Season: Comes inshore from spring to early autumn, and is most common in the English Channel and around the southern and western coasts of Ireland.

Haunts: Nomadic.

Feeding Habits: Diet includes whitebait and other small fry.

Fishing Methods: Often taken by shore and boat anglers with lures and baits intended for mackerel. Light float fishing from a pier, harbour wall or rock is a popular method.

Baits: Mackerel slip, whitebait, mussel.

• SHARKS

Four species of shark are of interest to British big game anglers—the blue shark, the porbeagle, the mako, and the thresher.

The Blue Shark is found mainly around the coasts of south-west England, south-west Wales, and south-west

Sea Fish A.B.C.

Ireland. The body is very dark blue on the back, becoming paler on the sides and white underneath. Sometimes, in pursuit of mackerel shoals, blue shark come very close in to steep-to shingle beaches, but normally they are found well out to sea. British rod-caught record: 218 lb. (Looe, 1959).

The Porbeagle and Mako Sharks are very similar, and both attain a greater size than the blue shark. They are grey or brownish on the back, shading to white underneath. The Porbeagle is found off the Isle of Wight, Channel Islands, South-west England and west coast of Ireland. Mako sharks are mostly encountered in Cornish and neighbouring waters. Distinguishing Features: Porbeagle—pectoral fin overlaps first dorsal fin; teeth have small accessory cusps at the base. Mako—pectoral fin does not overlap first dorsal fin; teeth are irregularly arranged with no accessory cusps. British rod-caught records: Porbeagle—430 lb. (S. of Jersey, 1969); Mako—500 lb. (off Eddystone Light, 1971).

The Thresher Shark is not captured so frequently as the previously mentioned species, but gives good sport. It can be easily recognised by its remarkable tail—the upper lobe of which is very nearly as long as its body. These sharks, often hunting in pairs, will sometimes 'round up' a shoal of mackerel, pilchards or other fish by threshing the water with their tails—hence their name. British rod-caught record: 280 lb. (Dungeness, 1933).

Fishing Methods: Shark fishing is nearly always carried on from a boat; usually, but not invariably, a considerable distance offshore. On most British coasts the season extends throughout the summer until September or October, depending on the weather and other conditions.

Special big game tackle is necessary to capture the larger sharks, comprising a specially designed shark rod and reel, and shoulder harness. At most recognised shark angling centres it is possible to hire suitable tackle from the local tackle dealers, whilst the boatmen supply bait, any necessary advice or instruction, and the large gaffs necessary for boating the fish.

In areas where only modest-sized blue shark are expected, however, there is no reason why an angler should not try his luck with a medium boat rod and multiplier reel. It is recommended that the reel be loaded with 250—300 yards of non-stretch braided terylene line.

In skilled hands, even a medium fibreglass boat rod can be used to play out blue shark up to 90 lb. or so, because fibreglass will not take on a 'set' when subjected to prolonged strain, and is capable of taking a great deal of punishment in its stride.

The terminal tackle consists of a long and adequately swivelled cable-laid wire trace, carrying a good quality forged hook about 2 in. across the bend.

Sea anglers who own their own motor launch, and live on a suitable coast, could easily cope with the general run of blue shark. A good working plan is to catch some mackerel for bait on a feathered trace, and then suspend the bait from a large float at the same depth as the mackerel were caught.

The boat is allowed to drift, and at the same time a small-meshed net bag of mashed-up mackerel, pilchard or other oily fish is suspended overboard. As the boat drifts it leaves behind it an attractive trail of fish oil and blood, and any sharks in the area will follow up this scent.

When a shark takes the bait, let it run for a little way; then strike *hard* to drive the big hook home. Meanwhile, other anglers in the boat must reel in their lines immediately.

When the fish is played out, gaff it near the tail, and if necessary, slip a rope noose around the tail.

° SKATE AND RAYS

Many sea anglers despise the sporting possibilities of skate, possibly taking their cue from Bickerdyke, who once declared that pumping up one of these large kite-shaped fish was like playing an animated dining-room table.

This is perfectly true; yet even an animated dining-room table can be the cause of quite a lot of excitement when attached reluctantly to the end of one's line!

Sea Fish A.B.C.

Skate fishing can be divided conveniently into two categories, as follows: (a) Fishing with heavy tackle for 100 lb.-plus common skate, white skate and long-nosed skate; (b) fishing with a medium boat outfit for thornback rays weighing as a rule about 8 to 15 pounds. Other modest-sized species are the blonde ray, painted (or small-eyed) ray, undulate ray, cuckoo ray, etc., but these are more localised than the thornback.

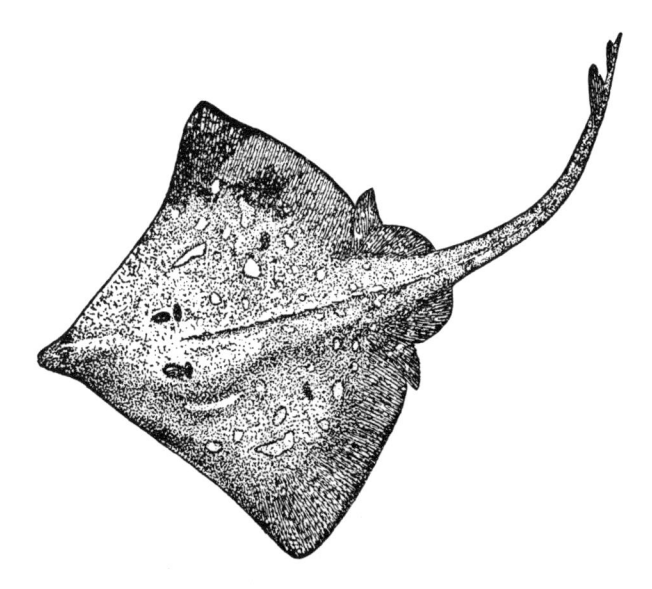

The Common Skate is usually brown or grey on the upper side, with lighter markings, and greyish with variable black markings underneath. Caught mostly on rod and line off W. Ireland and N. Scotland. Has been caught commercially to well over 400 lb. British rod-caught record: 226 lb. 8 oz. (Shetland, 1970).

The Thornback Ray is a much smaller species, and derives its name from the thornlike spines on its back and tail. The upper side is mottled brown, and the underside is white. It is found all round the British Isles. British rod-caught record: 38 lb. (Rustington Beach, 1935).

Haunts: Common Skate—often found on mixed ground

of sand and rock. Thornback—sandy or gravelly areas, often quite close inshore, or in estuaries.

Feeding Habits: Common Skate—preys on bottom fish, lobsters, various kinds of crabs, shrimps, etc. Thornback—small flatfish, sandeels, hermit crabs, shrimps, etc.

Shore Fishing Methods: The thornback is the species most commonly taken by the shore and pier angler. It may be caught on all sorts of ground tackle, but best results are likely to be obtained with a leger carrying a single round-bend hook, about size 4/0.

Boat Fishing Methods: A powerful, short-butted rod is a 'must' when fishing for large skate—also a strong reel, a 50—80 lb. breaking strain braided line, a leger lead running on the line, and a 3 ft. wire trace attached by a strong swivel link to a single forged steel hook mounted on a 12 in. wire snood.

If you are fishing for thornback rays in an area where big skate are unlikely to be encountered, you may safely omit the wire trace and use instead a 5/0 hook tied direct to a 3 ft. trace of 50 lb. b.s. braided terylene.

This lighter form of terminal tackle makes for pleasanter fishing, and the braided trace will be capable of holding the large conger which are occasionally hooked when night fishing for rays.

The 'bite' of a skate when boat fishing is often not a bite at all, but the impact of the large, flat body flopping down on the line. The strike should therefore be delayed, and I find that counting up to ten gives the fish time to mouth the bait properly, without allowing it to take the hook down too far so that disgorging it later on becomes a messy and troublesome business.

Catches are usually improved if, before arriving on the fishing ground, a net bag is hitched on to the anchor rope. This is filled with chopped-up mackerel flesh and guts, or pulped herring and sprats, according to season. It is best to position it about 8 ft. above the sea-bed, because if attached lower than this dogfish sometimes start tearing at it.

The size of hook used for common skate will naturally

Sea Fish A.B.C.

depend on the type of bait used. Some anglers go up to 10/0, using a whole mackerel or herring. This, however, is suitable mainly for areas where really big specimens are expected. On most inshore marks one obtains better results with a 5/0 to 7/0 hook (round-bend sizes), baited generously with a large slice of mackerel, frozen herring, squid, or a whole sprat or small harvest mackerel. Peeler crab is also useful; while in some areas thornback rays eagerly accept large prawns.

Night fishing produces the best results.

STING RAY

A member of the skate family which comes close inshore in summer or early autumn, when it is caught by anglers fishing from beach, pier or boat. It is mainly encountered along certain stretches of coastline in southern, south-western and south-eastern England.

These fish, which run to a considerable size, are armed with a venomous spine in the tail, which can be slashed furiously back and forth.

A hefty blow between the eyes with the proverbial blunt instrument should kill the fish, but it cannot be considered safe until the tail has been cut off, or the sting removed with a pair of pliers. To do this, turn the fish upside down and hold the tail down firmly with your boot.

DON'T leave the sting lying around where it may be handled by children, or trodden on by bare-footed swimmers.

British rod-caught record: 59 lb. (Clacton-on-Sea, 1952).

SOLE

This very tasty flatfish has an oval body, brown or greyish with black blotches on the upper side, and white underneath. There is a black tip to the upper pectoral fin. British rod-caught record: 4 lb. 1 oz. 14 dr. (Guernsey, 1967).

Location and Season: Mainly found around the southern half of the British Isles, including Ireland. Most likely to be taken on rod and line in summer.

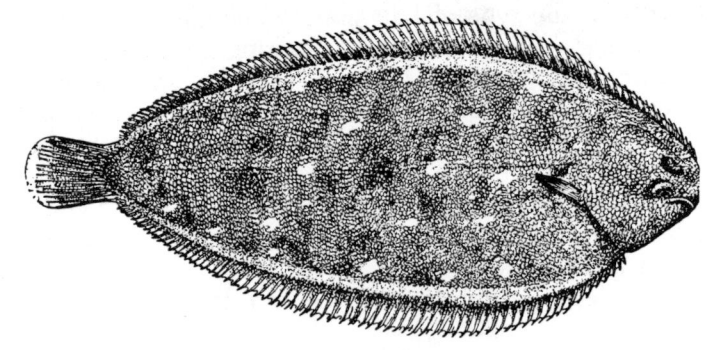

Haunts: Muddy or sandy areas, and on soft ground amongst scattered rocks.
Feeding Habits: Feeds on the bottom on marine worms, shrimps, razor fish and starfish.
Fishing Methods: Light monofilament leger or paternoster-trot from boat, pier or shore. Catches are usually best at night.
Baits: Ragworm, lugworm, razorfish.

° TOPE

Every year this smallish member of the shark family becomes more popular with the British sea angler, and not for nothing is it sometimes referred to as 'the dinghy angler's big game fish'.

It is capable of providing excellent sport; yet at the same time does not call for any outlay on expensive special tackle, or the hiring of a deep-sea boat and its crew.

The tope is mainly brownish or greyish in colour, becoming white underneath. British rod-caught record: 74 lb. 11 oz. (Caldy Island, 1964).

Location and Season: More common and widely distributed than is generally realised. The Thames Estuary, many parts of the English Channel, Pembrokeshire, and the Irish Sea are all productive tope areas. Mainly taken in summer and early autumn.

Haunts: Tope are usually found in areas of sand or shell-grit, but they often come close in to rocky headlands, or explore reefs jutting up out of a sandy area.

Sea Fish A.B.C.

Feeding Habits: Preys on small flatfish, whiting, bream, etc., and therefore usually swims fairly close to the bottom.

Shore Fishing: Although most tope fishing is carried on from boats, it is possible on certain parts of the coast to capture this fish from the shore. Very often these shore-caught specimens are of excellent size.

Tackle varies for this type of fishing, but one useful set-up consists of a 4 ft. trace of 30—50 lb. b.s. plastic-covered cable-laid stainless wire carrying a 6/0 hook at one end and a swivel at the other end. This swivel is tied to the reel line, on which slides a free-running lead. The reel (a beachcasting multiplier) should hold about 250—300 yards of 20 lb. b.s. nylon monofilament, but to the end of this I blood-knot about 7 yards of stronger 28 lb. b.s. monofilament.

The reason for using a wire trace is that tope sometimes roll themselves on the line, which is then liable to become frayed against the fish's rough hide. However, when long-distance casting is necessary from the shore, many very successful tope anglers accept this risk, and attach the wire hook link and swivel direct to the reel line.

Fish baits are used, and many tope anglers fishing from the shore favour a large piece of frozen herring. This, on a 5/0 hook, is also well within the capabilities of any large bass, conger or huss which may be around. Mackerel (especially the small 'harvest' mackerel) are also very good.

It should be mentioned that most tope insist on a tidy-looking bait, and that as little as possible of the hook should be visible. Whether or not the point should be left exposed is a controversial detail, but if it *is* hidden it should be buried only very lightly, and slanted so that it pulls clear of the bait as soon as the strike is made.

The bite of a tope varies considerably. Very often line suddenly starts to scream off the reel, and the fish may continue its initial run for ten seconds or more. Then comes a pause. It is a mistake to strike until the fish starts to move off for the SECOND time.

By way of contrast, some tope swim inshore after picking up the bait, so you must always be prepared for a slack-line bite. In these circumstances, you must reel in slack line as quickly as possible until contact is made with the fish; then delay the strike until you feel it heading away from you.

Boat Fishing: The terminal tackle may be similar to that recommended for shore fishing, except that the trace should preferably be somewhat longer—say 6–7 ft. Personally, however, I prefer to use a 6-ft. trace of 80 lb. b.s. *nylon monofilament* terminating in a swivelled 12-inch link of cable-laid wire carrying a 6/0 or 7/0 hook. This arrangement makes the bait feel lighter and more natural to the tope when it mouths the bait.

Any medium-powered glass-fibre boat rod can be used for tope, and this should be matched with a medium-capacity multiplier reel. Line strength will naturally depend to a large degree upon the power curve of the rod, but for the newcomer to tope fishing something in the region of 30 lb. b.s. would be about right. There is, however, plenty of scope for lighter tackle in skilled hands. My own preference is for a non-stretch line of braided terylene or dacron, as this makes for more positive striking when the fish is a long way from the boat.

Suitable baits include a whole freshly-caught mackerel, threaded head-first on to the wire hook-link with a baiting needle; or, alternatively, a large fillet of mackerel on a slightly smaller hook.

Tope are usually fished for from an anchored boat, and the commonest method is legering on the bottom. Bait, trace and line are streamed out astern into the tide, but the lead is retained in the hand until about four full arm-spans of line have been paid out into the water.

Then the lead is 'stopped' with a sliver of matchstick fastened to the line with a clove-hitch; after which the lead is lowered overboard until it touches bottom.

The idea of this arrangement, of course, is that on reeling in, or playing a fish, the piece of matchstick will break upon pressure from the end-ring of the rod, and the lead

Sea Fish A.B.C.

will slide out of the way, until it fetches up against the trace swivel.

Tope fishing is a waiting game, but when a 'run' comes it is a thrilling experience. As the reel screams, and line starts pouring off the spool, you must guard against the temptation to strike prematurely. If using a large whole fish bait, wait until the tope pauses and then commences its second run before driving home the hook.

Tope have an awkward habit of getting round the anchor rope. If you have a companion with you he can haul the anchor aboard, but as a lone angler I like to have the rope buoyed with a couple of pot corks, and let it slip if things get hectic. One quick pull at a slippery hitch does the trick, but the corks, of course, must be outboard of the fairlead. Under such circumstances, though, it is as well to have a spare rope and anchor aboard.

Baits: Mackerel and herring (whole or fillets), whiting, dab (rolled and trussed, 'blind' side outermost).

Note: Anglers frequently confuse the Smooth Hound with the Tope. The main difference is that the tope has much sharper teeth—small, triangular and serrated on the cutting edge. The smooth hound has flattened teeth, and there are often some light-coloured spots on its upper side.

TUNNY

Imagine a mackerel weighing a quarter of a ton, and you have a rough idea of what a decent-sized tunny looks like! In fact sometimes these fish attain almost double that weight.

Until the late 1930's tunny were being caught on rod and line many miles out in the North Sea—the centres for this rugged form of big game fishing being Scarborough and Whitby. Even in those days it was an expensive sport, and today rising costs and a decrease in the number of tunny has put an end to this very exciting sport.

British rod-caught record: 851 lb. (North Sea, 1933).

° TURBOT

This flatfish attains a considerable size, and on certain

coasts is highly prized by anglers. Its body is mottled and speckled brown on the back, and covered with small bony lumps known as tubercles. The underside is white. British rod-caught record: 31 lb. 4 oz. (off Eddystone, 1972).

Location and Season: Found mainly around the English and Irish Coasts from May to September. Rather localised. Some noted turbot marks are the Varne Bank, off Folkestone; the Shambles Bank, Weymouth, and the Skerries Bank, near Dartmouth.

Haunts: Lives mainly on the bottom in areas of sand or shell-grit. Sometimes ventures quite close inshore, and is frequently found in the vicinity of submerged estuarial and near-shore sandbanks.

Feeding Habits: Preys on small bottom fish, and is particularly fond of sandeels.

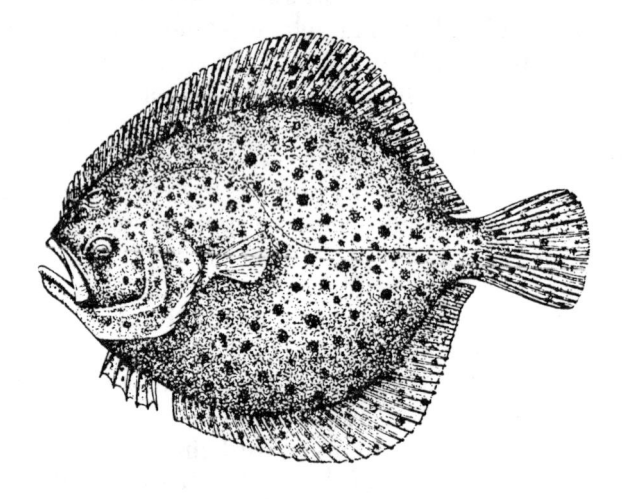

Shore Fishing: Turbot are not often specially fished for from the shore, but they are occasionally taken by pier and beach fishermen when using fish baits. A likely vantage point is near the entrance to a sandy estuary—the bait being cast out into the deep-water channel.

Boat Fishing: (i) Fishing at anchor with a live sandeel on a monofilament leger or paternoster-trot. (ii) Slow drifting

Sea Fish A.B.C.

with the bait tripping along the sea-bed on a long, light trace.

Baits: Live sandeel, mackerel strips, live poor cod, fresh sprats.

WEEVER

For their own protection, sea anglers should familiarise themselves with the two species of weever found in British waters. Armed with venomous spines situated in the first dorsal fin and on the gill covers, they are quite capable of ruining a holiday if handled carelessly. Indeed, there have even been cases—fortunately rare—in which a

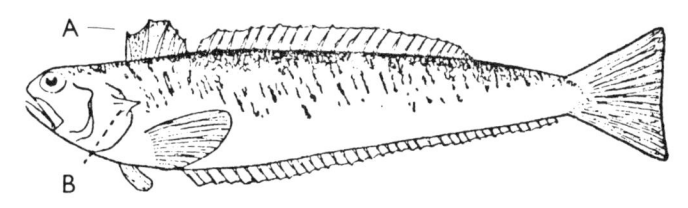

Fig. 35. The Greater Weever, showing venomous spines.

prick from one of those poisonous spines has proved fatal.

The Greater Weever is the more virulent species. An offshore variety, it is most likely to be caught by boat anglers when fishing fairly deep water. The body is predominantly yellowish-brown, with darker oblique markings on the sides. British rod-caught record: 2 lb. 4 oz. (Brighton, 1927).

The Lesser Weaver, as its name implies, is a much smaller fish, measuring as a rule when full-grown some 5—7 inches. This gives it a plumper appearance than the Greater Weever depicted in Fig. 35, but otherwise it possesses the main characteristics of its larger relative.

It frequents sandy inshore shallows, lying partially buried on the sea-bed—a menace to swimmers and anglers alike.

When a weever is caught, it should be pinned down with

the gaff handle, killed by stabbing it in the head with a long-bladed knife, and the hook carefully cut free. When boat fishing some distance from land, the body can then be picked up by impaling it on the knife blade, and tossed overboard.

However, as the spines remain poisonous long after death, the fish should be disposed of carefully when shore fishing.

WHITING

This slim-bodied member of the cod family is bronze-brown on the back, shading to a silvery colour on the lower sides and underneath. British rod-caught record: 6 lb. 3 oz. 3 dr. (off Rame Head, 1971).

Location and Season: Found around most parts of the British Isles. The shoals are likely to be encountered inshore in autumn and winter.

Haunts and Food: Usually swims close to the bottom in areas of sand or muddy sand, but will swim upwards to other levels or enter rocky areas when hunting. Diet includes small herrings and pilchards, sprats, whitebait, poor cod, sandeels, shrimps, pouting, marine worms—and smaller whiting.

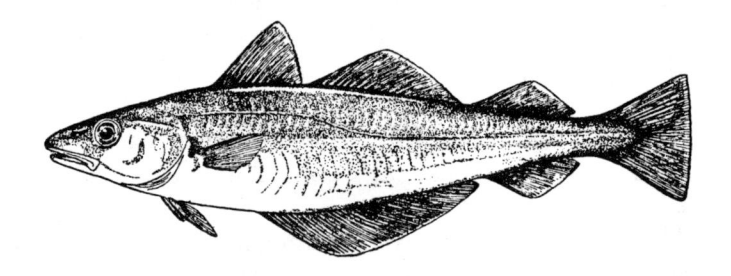

Shore Fishing Methods: During the late autumn and winter months, whiting are caught by casting out a light monofilament paternoster from pier-head or open beach. The best catches are made towards sundown and after nightfall, often in frosty weather. Suitable hooks vary between sizes 1—4, depending upon the size and mood of the fish, and the type of bait being used.

Sea Fish A.B.C.

Boat Fishing Methods: (i) Drifting with a monofilament paternoster trace carrying two or three transparent plastic booms. (ii) Same tackle used from an anchored boat. (iii) When fish are shy, driftlining 'deep and steep' with a light, single-hook flowing trace.

When boat fishing by any of the above methods, it is helpful to lower to the fishing depth a weighted net bag filled with mashed-up oily fish.

Hooks as a rule should be as recommended for shore fishing, but in daylight, when the water is clear, it may be necessary to use very small baits on size 6 hooks.

Baits: Thin strips of sprat, herring, pilchard and whiting; whitebait, mussel, ragworm, lugworm, raw shrimp and hermit crab.

WRASSE

The Ballan Wrasse is the species of wrasse most commonly caught in British waters. It is also the largest. Coloration is variable, but is usually reddish-brown or greenish-brown on the back, tinged with blue, and becoming lighter on the sides and whitish below. The lips are very thick, and teeth very large—giving this fish a resemblance to the traditional 'nigger minstrel'. British rod-caught record: 7 lb. 10 oz. 15 dr. (off Trevose Head, 1970).

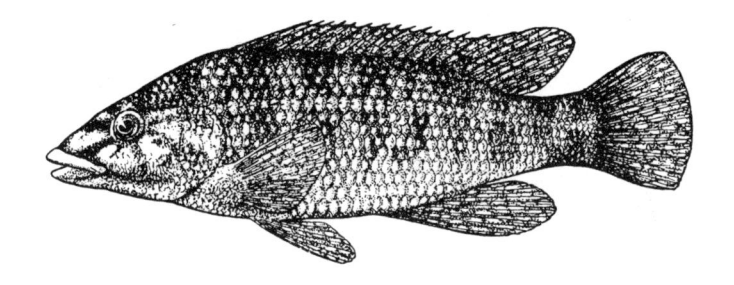

The Cuckoo Wrasse is more slender-bodied than the above, and is very colourful. The male is a vivid orangy-gold, with bright blue patches and lines; the female is mostly red with a few black spots along the back.

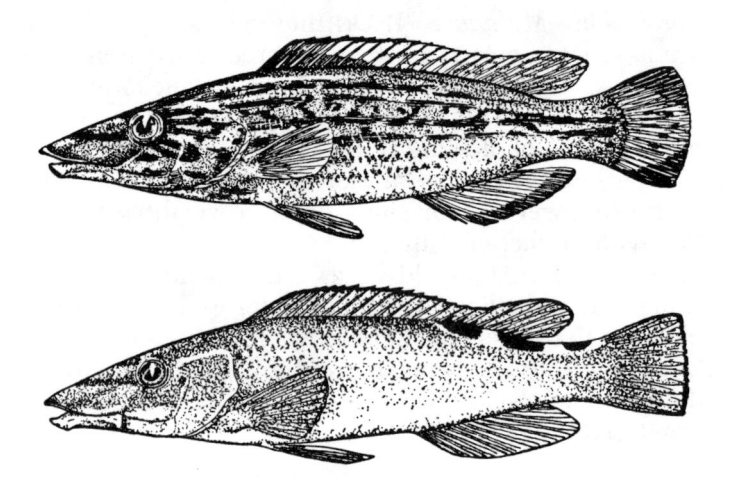

The Corkwing Wrasse is the smallest species of wrasse commonly taken on rod and line. It rarely exceeds 8 or 9 inches, and is of no particular interest to the angler.

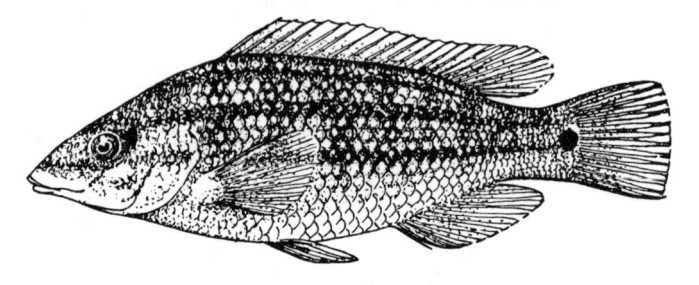

Location and Season: The ballan wrasse is found around most parts of the British Isles. The cuckoo wrasse is rather more localised, and is encountered more often around our southern and south-western coasts.
Haunts: Swims near the bottom in rocky, weedy areas.
Feeding Habits: Diet includes small crabs, shellfish and prawns.
Shore Fishing: Not often fished for deliberately, but often caught on sliding float tackle fished deep from a rock or stone harbour breakwater. Also taken on ground tackle cast out on to sand very close to rocky ground.

Sea Fish A.B.C.

A wrasse must be reeled in as quickly as possible, because as soon as it feels the hook it will try to swim into the nearest gap or crevice in the rocks.
Boat Fishing: Often taken when driftlining or paternostering close to rocks for other species.
Baits: Ragworm, prawns, peeler crabs.

CHAPTER 10

Baits

THE following alphabetical list of salt-water baits will be found particularly useful by holiday anglers visiting the quieter stretches of coast, where commercial bait dealers are non-existent. Where applicable, the angler is told how to discover or catch these baits, and information is also given on the best methods of placing them on the hook.

Boulder Eels were a favourite bait of the old-time professional longshore fishermen, who used them when trolling for pollack and bass. They are actually tiny river and conger eels, and their chief merit is that they are often present on shores where sandeels are unobtainable.

Any muddy shore that is littered with small boulders at low tide is likely to provide a supply, but these eels are usually most numerous where fresh water from a stream trickles down the foreshore into the sea. Those about 4½— 6 in. long are the most convenient size for bait, and they can be found by turning over boulders which have a broad, flattish base.

When present, the eels reveal themselves by wriggling vigorously towards the nearest tide-pool or clump of weed. They are very slippery and difficult to grasp in the fingers, so most bait hunters use an old table-fork to pin them down.

When used for trolling or spinning, the eel is first killed, and the point of a round-bend, long-shanked hook inserted into the mouth. The eel's body is then coaxed up the shank of the hook until the hook-eye has disappeared well inside its mouth. A short length of thread is then twisted and knotted around the eel's 'throat' to prevent the body slipping back down the shank when being drawn through the

Baits

water; the hook-point meanwhile having been brought out again underneath the eel.

Boulder eels can also be used as a livebait, and when presented on a driftline they often meet with a ready response from estuary bass. For this type of fishing a medium-shank, fine-wire hook can be snicked through the back, a little behind the head.

Bream. Strips from a scaled red or black bream will tempt big pollack; whilst a fillet or small whole fish is good for conger, skate, huss, tope and various other species.

Cockles are a useful bait for plaice, dabs, wrasse, pouting and whiting. They are commonly found in estuaries, and can be obtained by scraping with a rake or hoe close to the low tide line on shores of sand or sandy mud.

Hermit Crab. This sea-bed creature looks rather like a tiny, shell-less lobster, and it obtains protection from its enemies by setting up home in an empty whelk shell. It is a scavenger, and in some areas is a common find in lobster pots and baited drop-nets. The fleshy tail portion makes an excellent bait for flatfish, pouting and whiting. Used whole, but with the claws removed, it is also good for bass, cod and thornback ray.

Herring strips and cuttings are a useful bait for bass, conger, skate, dogfish, whiting, cod, pollack, coalfish, etc., and large fillets are also much used for tope. In recent years the packeted brands of deep-frozen herring have become tremendously popular with beach fishermen, and there is no doubt that they are 'fresher' (and therefore a better bait) than herring bought off the fishmonger's slab. Methods of baiting up are similar to those recommended for mackerel.

Limpets are common on most rocky coasts, but unfortunately do not make a very good bait. However, when nothing better is available they can be used for wrasse and red bream. Use the soft upper part of the shellfish, with just enough of the tough 'foot' to keep it on the hook.

Slipper Limpets should not be confused with ordinary rock limpets. These are a first-class bait for bass and flatfish, but they normally live beyond the low tide line. In some areas they are dredged up in their thousands by oyster fishermen, and may also be found on certain shores around low spring tides, or after a gale.

Lugworms. On any flat and reasonably sheltered expanse of tide-swept sand one can expect to find a colony of lugworms. This very useful sea bait is particularly common in shallow sandy bays which are protected from the prevailing westerly winds, and in estuaries where a certain amount of mud is mixed with the sand.

There are several different kinds of lugworm, but from the bait-digger's point of view they can be divided into two categories—the common type which lives in U-shaped burrows, and those which burrow straight down.

The Common Lugworm

Around low tide the most productive digging grounds are revealed by the familiar 'casts' thrown up by these worms. Upon making a closer inspection, the novice digger will also notice that for every cast there is a small funnel-shaped hole in the sand—referred to on some parts of the coast as 'lug dupples' or 'dimples'.

The lugworm lies between these two points in a U-shaped burrow; usually within a foot or so of the surface, although the average depth may vary considerably from one bait ground to another. A useful tool for digging them out is a broad-tined gardening fork. A spade is not recommended for *this* type of lugworm, because it is likely to chop many of them in half.

The method of digging varies according to local conditions, and on thinly populated bait grounds it usually saves a lot of hard work if the worms are dug individually. This is done by selecting a cast and dupple, and thrusting the fork into the sand alongside the estimated run of the burrow. Sometimes, if the worms are lying shallow, and the fork has long tines, it may only be necessary to lift one forkful of sand for each worm.

Normally, however, it will be necessary to go down two spits, in a vertical direction, before slanting the fork beneath the estimated position of the worm and lifting it out.

Baits

As a rule the largest worms are found beneath those casts and dupples which are widest apart. Also, it is reasonably safe to assume that these big worms will be lying fairly deep.

In a thickly populated bait ground a more rewarding method is 'patch digging'. This is best done by opening up a narrow strip of likely-looking sand, then digging backwards from it, using the sand just extracted to fill the strip previously excavated.

Don't leave your bait-digging patch looking like an open-cast mine. On a sheltered shore it may take several tides to fill in these holes, which meanwhile remain a trap for the unwary when covered with water. For a boatman it may mean only a boot full of water, but for a small child it could be much more dangerous.

When digging lug, the bait-box should have at least two roomy, pitch-lined partitions—one for uninjured worms; the other for those which have been damaged by the fork. Use the damaged ones first.

On some lug grounds it is not unusual to come across small ragworms, and a third partition in the bait-box will be an advantage. Never mix lugworm with ragworm.

Incidentally, it is not always an advantage to dig the largest lug. It is true that the big ones are best for bass and cod, but for dabs, plaice and flounders it is the small to medium-sized ones which give best results. Lugworms also make a good bait for whiting, pouting, wrasse and bream.

When lug are plentiful, as they usually are when present at all, there is little point in using the tail of the worm. This, being full of sand, has little attraction for fish.

The remainder of the worm can be threaded on a long-shank, round-bend hook, bringing the hook-point out again fairly low down so that about an inch of the worm is left dangling.

On some lug grounds the worms are very short and stubby, and it may then be necessary to bait up with two or three at a time. With their tails nipped off, these can often be threaded one behind the other on a long-shanked hook, with yet another dangling from the bend of the hook.

Lugworm lack the remarkable vitality of ragworm, and there is little point in trying to keep them alive for more than two or three days. My own experience is that dark-coloured worms keep better than the light-coloured varieties. Those not intended for use on the day of digging should be placed in a roomy shallow box on a layer of clean, dry newspaper, and then covered with another sheet of newspaper. On no account should they be overcrowded.

The 'Straight-Down' Lugworm

This type of lugworm varies in colour. At Skegness, for example, those halfway up the beach are inclined to be red, brown or orange, but around the limits of low spring tides they are black. Worms around 18 in. long are not uncommon.

The most suitable tool for digging this type of worm is a farmer's draining spade, with a 10 in. blade tapering from 4 in. to 2½ in. in width. However, an ordinary garden spade will do provided it has a long, narrow blade.

The first indication the visiting angler has that he is up against this type of lugworm is the fact that, although the beach is covered with plenty of tail casts, there are no head holes, or dupples.

Digging for these 'straight-down' worms is an energetic business, and both speed and care are essential. It would appear that the moment one begins digging, the worm starts to go down. This it can do pretty quickly, because it doesn't have to 'eat' its way into the sand—its burrow is already made.

The aim of the digger is to follow the hole downwards, and it is a good plan to drag the spade across the hole when removing this part of the sand. This action turns the tail part of the worm from vertical, thus halting its downward progress.

As soon as the worm is glimpsed, one should reach down into the sand and grasp it as far down the body as possible. This is not always easy, but the sand is usually wet

Baits

and mushy at this depth, and by wriggling one's outstretched fingers and hand it is usually possible to get a fair way down into the sand.

It is important at this stage to withdraw the worm gently without trying to hurry matters. Unfortunately, there is a temptation to hurry, because on most shores water soon begins to seep into the hole, and sometimes the edge on which one is kneeling begins to crumble. As far as is possible, sand removed from the hole should be used to prevent the water rushing in.

Incidentally, when a digger sees a tail cast with a clear hole through it, the worm is usually just under the surface, instead of being perhaps a couple of feet down. The average depth of the 'straight-down' lugworm varies to some extent from coast to coast, but almost invariably it is found farther down than the kinds which live in U-shaped burrows. In some places I have even had to dig three feet to get them.

A rather odd thing about this type of lugworm is that if handled roughly, or damaged slightly, its head slowly swells until it bursts, throwing out guts and blood, often to a distance of several feet. This is an advantage—provided one does not get in the line of fire!—because after blowing its top, the body of the worm becomes firm and tough.

In this condition it stays well on the hook, and can be used in small sections. It can also be salted down.

Mackerel are a popular bait on many coasts during the summer and autumn months, but for best results they should be used fresh from the sea. Shop-bought mackerel are always a bit 'tired', even when purchased in a coastal town.

The method of baiting up varies. Whole mackerel are used for shark and tope; while small harvest mackerel also have a strong appeal for tope and sizable common skate, large huss or conger. Normally, however, in areas where the last three species run to a more modest size, one would fillet the mackerel and bait up with large portions.

Smaller strips, about ½—¾ in. wide, are also a good bait

for bass, turbot, thornback, skate, pollack, pouting, whiting, cod, scad, garfish and other mackerel. The strips vary in length according to the species and mood of the fish. When an extra long strip is required (perhaps as a spinning bait) this may be cut diagonally from the side of the fish.

Strip baits used for ground fishing or deep driftlining are often twisted around the hook shank, after which a short piece is left dangling below the bend. A point to be noted, however, is that when driftlining this twist tends to make the bait revolve in a flow of tide. This may make the bait more attractive, but it also necessitates using a swivel and anti-kink lead if line-twist is to be avoided.

For trolling, however, I prefer to use an untwisted bait, mounted on two hooks as illustrated in Fig. 36.

Small mackerel cuttings are useful when float fishing for bass, mackerel, scad, pollack and garfish, but it is important to trim the thickness of the cutting with a sharp knife, as well as their length and breadth.

Finally, for those who hanker to catch a real rod-bender, it is worth mentioning that many big fish—particularly bass and monkfish—have been taken on ground tackle baited with a mackerel head. If the head is pulled off, so that the guts are left trailing, this is said to make the bait more attractive.

This sort of bait should be presented on a fairly long trace, and because its appeal is limited it is best used (when ground fishing) on two-hook tackle carrying also a smaller strip bait.

Mussels. With its slate-blue shell, and its habit of clinging in closely packed colonies to harbour walls, pier piles and crevice-pocked rocks, the mussel is too familiar to require description. It is probably our most widely distributed and commonly used shellfish bait, and is first-class for codling, whiting, pouting, bream, wrasse and small to medium-sized coalfish. In many districts it is also taken readily by plaice and dabs.

Mussels vary considerably in size according to their

Baits

situation, and for most kinds of fishing the large ones will be found most suitable.

If you live near a sheltered harbour, estuary, creek or sea-loch, you can keep the mussels in a sack or courge immersed in the water. Alternatively, if you live on an exposed coast, you can keep them in a cool outhouse, in an old earthenware sink filled with sea water. Provided you change the water once or twice, they will remain alive for a fortnight or more.

Fig. 36. Hook set-up for trolling with fish-strips.

There is a knack in opening mussels so that they can be baited up neatly. The first essential is a knife with a stubby but well-tempered blade. The one I use is a broken table-knife, re-shaped on an emery wheel as shown in Fig. 37.

Now, assuming you are right-handed, hold the mussel firmly in your left hand, so that it is lying horizontally with its blunt end (A in the drawing) towards you, and side B facing the knife in your right hand. With the cutting edge of the knife clean away any of the mussel's 'anchor threads' which may be still adhering to the shell. This will reveal a slight indentation at the join of the shell, and here you should insert the chisel edge of the knife.

By thrusting and wiggling the knife to and fro you will get the end of the blade inside the shell. At the same time, tilt the blade so that it enters the upper half of the shell between the mussel flesh and the inner face of the shell. The flesh, you will notice, is attached to each rim of the shell by a gristly fringe, which is sometimes referred to as the 'lips'.

With a slicing motion, coax the cutting edge of the knife around the blunt end of the shell, so that it separates the gristly lips from the rim of its shell. Suddenly, after rounding the end of the shell, you will feel something 'give', and you will know that you have severed the muscle which has hitherto been keeping the shell tightly closed.

It is now a simple matter to slice (with the cutting edge) and scoop (with the chisel-edge) the mussel flesh out of the two halves of the shell in one piece.

Some anglers use a double-edged knife so that the blade can be run around inside the shell in both directions without removing it. Personally I don't like this sort of tool, because I like to press my forefinger against the back of the knife to steady and guide it, and to regulate the depth of insertion.

Anyway, there is no need to withdraw the blade until the muscle has been severed, and then, with the shell gaping, there is no difficulty in withdrawing the knife and slicing round the other end (C) of the shell.

Mussel flesh is rather soft, so care must be taken when baiting up. Use a fine-wire hook, and thrust the point first of all through the dark-brown or yellowish protrusion situated between the two lobes of the mussel.

Near where the lobes join there is also some reasonably firm flesh—pass the hook through this as well, and then turn the hook and pass it through the gristly disc of muscle.

It is not a bad idea, especially when beach casting, to open up a good supply of mussels and spread them out on the lid of the bait-box for about an hour. This will help to make them firmer. Don't expose them for longer than an hour, because the bait then seems to lose some of its attraction for fish.

Baits

For the same reason it is also a mistake to open mussels the lazy man's way—by dropping them into boiling water—even though this also hardens the flesh and makes baiting up much easier.

If local conditions make it absolutely essential to use a firm bait, a more satisfactory method is to put the mussels into a pan and just cover them with cold water. Warm the water slowly and, when the shells open, remove the flesh. Some anglers then anoint the mussels with pilchard oil while still warm; in which case they should be placed in a screw-topped glass or plastic jar—not a wooden bait-box.

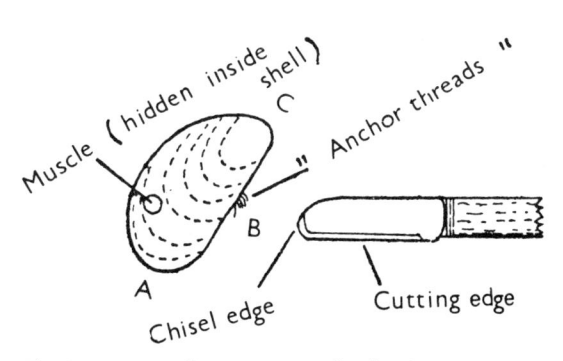

Fig. 37. Diagram showing method of opening mussels.

Peeler and Soft Crabs. The familiar greenish-brown shore crab features prominently in the diet of many sea fish, but normally its hard shell limits its usefulness as a hook bait. At intervals in the natural process of growing, however, every crab sheds its shell—whereupon, like a generously proportioned matron relieved of her corsets, its body increases rapidly in size. Then the skin hardens to form a new protective shell.

Immediately after moulting, the crab's soft body is easily placed on a hook, and makes an ideal bait for bass, flounders, pollack, codling, wrasse, thornback skate and many other species. In this condition it is known as a 'soft' crab. A crab which is on the point of shedding its shell is known as a 'peeler'.

All this is common knowledge, and it is mainly the practical business of finding a sufficient quantity of peeler and soft crabs which seems to puzzle novice sea anglers.

Obviously a crab without its shell is very vulnerable to predators. Therefore, as soon as one feels itself becoming a peeler, it goes into hiding.

It is rather an odd fact that, although hard-backed shore crabs are numerous on practically every coast, peeler or soft crabs can be found in numbers only along limited stretches of shore. The easiest place to find them is in a sheltered estuary, where a rocky promontory runs into firm mud near the low tide line. Rocks in such places are usually covered with bladder wrack, and the peeler and soft crabs can be found by flipping over the clumps of weed.

The discarded kettles and saucepans which inevitably collect on the bottom of a tidal harbour are also likely to yield peeler crabs. So are the crevices beneath rocks in sheltered tidal pools, but to haul them out you will probably need a 'crab-hook' made from a length of very stiff wire.

Peeler and soft crabs are usually most plentiful round about June, but on many coasts they can be found in reasonable numbers right through the summer and well into autumn.

Recognising peeler and soft crabs is not nearly so dificult as it is sometimes made out to be. The first thing to understand is that, for the hen crab, mating takes place shortly after the moulting process. However, some time before that (soon after becoming a peeler) she pairs off with a cock crab—who then has to carry her around everywhere in order to thwart her other ardent admirers.

On an estuary shore, searching for these paired crabs is the commonest method of finding peelers. The cock crab —which will be a useless hardback—adopts a pugilistic attitude when disturbed, but usually drops the peeler or soft hen as soon as he is picked up. To do this without getting your fingers nipped, grasp him across the carapace immediately behind his claws.

Baits

Cock crabs in the peeler or soft stage will be found hiding by themselves, and can usually be recognised by their lack of aggressiveness. Of course, a soft crab of either sex can also be identified by the soft rubbery feel of its body under finger pressure.

A recently moulted crab whose shell is only just beginning to harden is often referred to as a 'paper-back'. Its body also yields under finger pressure, but feels more like brown paper. It can be used as bait, but is not so good as a soft crab or peeler.

There are various other ways of identifying peeler and soft crabs. However, those already described are sufficient to obtain a good supply of bait on a suitable shoreline, and to go into greater detail would probably only confuse the novice.

To bait up with soft crab, first kill the crab by stabbing it in the head. Remove the claws and one of the legs. Pass the point of a fine-wire 4/0 hook through the leg socket and out through the middle of the back. Finally, secure the bait to the hook with a few twists of elasticated crimping thread.

Peeler crabs are dealt with in precisely the same way, except of course that the old shell must first be removed. When the crab is within a day or two of moulting, this can be done with a mere twist of the thumb-nail; but when the peeler stage is less advanced it is better to crack the shell gently around the edge before removing it.

Peeler crabs may be kept for quite a while in a courge floating at a mooring, or in a box filled with damp seaweed. They should be inspected daily, and any showing imminent signs of shedding their shells should be separated from the others. Soft crabs soon harden up, and should be used before the peelers.

Pilchard strips and cuttings are an excellent bait for bass, conger, dogfish, skate, whiting, cod and flounders, while small cuttings are also useful for grey mullet. Being rather soft, pilchard cuttings are not recommended for surf fishing, but they are suitable for boat work, float fishing, and short casting from rocks and harbour wall. As a rule freshly caught pilchards are only obtainable in Cornwall and West Devon.

Pouting and Poor-Cod. Many small fish, despised by the angler when they are caught on rod and line, can be used to tempt larger and more sporting species. For instance, one of the best baits for conger is a whole poor-cod or small pouting. A small live pouting, about 3 to 6 inches long, also makes an excellent bait for bass.

Similarly, medium-sized pouting can be used for tope, although it must be stressed that results with this bait vary from district to district. As a rough guide, it usually does best in places where the tope come in close to a reef or rocky headland.

Prawns are a first-class bait for bass, pollack, pouting, thornback skate, wrasse, gurnard, flounders and many other species. For bass or pollack it is best to use a live prawn on a fine-wire hook passed either upwards, or from side to side, through the scaly segment just in front of the tail. However, at very few places on the coast is it possible to buy live prawns from bait dealers or professional fishermen, and the sea angler usually has to catch his own.

On rugged coasts—particularly around Cornwall—prawns often become trapped at low tide among small rock pools, and it is then a simple matter to scoop them out with a hand-net. But tide-pool prawns are usually small, and it is the large ones (about 3—3½ in. long) which are most likely to catch big bass. These decent-sized prawns are found well down the littoral zone, and also beyond the limits of low tides.

Local conditions decide the methods used to catch them —the most common being (a) wading with a scoop-net, (b) wading with a push-net, (c) drop-netting from rocks, jetty, harbour wall or slipway, (d) drop-netting from a dinghy, and (e) setting prawn pots overnight.

For *daytime* prawning with baited drop-nets the water needs to be cloudy. One of the things which makes my own bit of coast a good prawning area is the fact that the local undercliffs are of blue lias, which discolours the sea inshore when washed out by waves or heavy rain. This pro-

Baits

vides the prawns with concealment from predatory fish, and gives them enough confidence to come to the baited nets in their dozens.

Similar conditions are encountered in or near tidal estuaries, where the water is usually discoloured by muddy drains and tributaries. Prawns are particularly plentiful in many West Country estuaries, and can be caught in baited drop-nets worked from stone revetments, jetties or a dinghy. Estuary prawns are also likely to be found close in to small promontories of weedy rock—especially when the rocks are surrounded by sand or mud just below the low tide level. The fisherman who wades around these rocks at low tide, thrusting a 3 ft. wide wooden-boomed push-net over the sand or mud, will often make some really large catches.

Among rocky pools and gullies on the open coast, the metal-framed type of prawning net is used. Down in the West Country we favour a net with a pear-shaped frame that is tilted upwards at a slight angle from the handle. The most profitable time to use this sort of net is during the last two hours or so of the ebb. One should follow the tide out as far as possible, thrusting under clumps of submerged weed attached to rocks, after which, with a quick upwards and backwards shaking movement, the net is withdrawn from the water, and any captured prawns transferred to the catch-bag. This bag should be fitted with a shoulder strap.

In much the same way the net can be thrust into rock crevices—pushing it in low down with the net frame tilted forwards and downwards, and withdrawing it high up against the roof of the crevice with the net tilted slightly backwards.

This form of hand-netting can be hard work, but for those who have learnt the knack it is usually the most likely method of getting a supply of prawns on a day when the water is clear.

When darkness falls, prawns will usually come to baited drop-nets whether the water be clear or cloudy, although their feeding habits are still governed by the tides. On my own coast we find that an outgoing tide gives best results, whether from rocks, jetty or dinghy; although after a lull at dead low water, things often buck up again during the first of the flood.

This state of affairs holds good on many other coasts, but it is not an invariable rule.

Bait for drop-nets presents no problems. A piece of kipper is excellent, because it gradually emits an attractively scented oil into the water. Mackerel, pouting, and cracked swimming and shore crabs are also very good. Kill the crabs first, of course.

Ragworms. Many different species of ragworm are found around the coasts of Britain, and collectively they form one of the most generally useful of sea baits. Not only do they appeal to a wide variety of fish, they are also easy to transport and keep alive, clean to handle, and stay on the hook well when casting.

The majority of large seaside tackle shops sell live ragworm during the holiday season. It is not a particularly cheap bait, however, and in suitable coastal areas the angler who can spare the time will have no difficulty in digging several days' supply in a single low tide.

For this task the requirements are a digging fork, a wooden bait-box with a broad base and close-fitting (but not airtight) lid, and a pair of wellington boots.

Normally, but not invariably, the best worms are found fairly close to the lowest limits of the tides.

In harbours and estuaries which dry out at low water to reveal an expanse of glutinous mud, it is common to find the small harbour ragworm. The very small ones, used singly, will take grey mullet, while those about 3 in. or more in length can be useful when float fishing for wrasse, school bass, inshore pollack and coalfish, or legering for flatfish.

Usually harbour ragworm do best when used two or three at a time. They can be bunched on a fine-wire hook, but very often a better method is to thread the first worm on to the hook, after which the remainder are suspended

Baits

from the bend by passing the hook-point through each worm near the head.

However, for ease of baiting and neatness of presentation, most anglers prefer something larger than the small harbour ragworm. This, in most districts, will be the 'medium-ragworm'—a rather loose term which is applied to various species averaging about 4½ in. to 7 in. in length.

These are found mostly on gently shelving shores consisting of closely-packed stones and mud. The depth at which they are found varies from coast to coast, but usually they will be somewhere between 6 in. to 18 in. down.

It is not always necessary to dig for ragworm. Quite often, by turning over small flat boulders lying on a mixture of stones and mud, you will surprise some very good ragworm actually resting on the surface. These should be grabbed without a second's delay, because they will immediately start to withdraw into their holes.

Don't squeeze a ragworm when you grab it. If it has to be pulled free, do so gently and steadily. If you try to hurry matters the worm will probably break in the middle, and the front half will continue crawling down into the mud.

Ragworm measuring about 7 in. to 1 ft. or more in length are generally referred to as king ragworm. These are much more limited in their distribution, but are dug in enormous quantities around the Solent.

Although king ragworm are a top bait in areas where they occur naturally, it is usually the medium-sized ragworm which appeals most to inshore fish in other districts.

When baiting up with a ragworm it should be held firmly just behind the head. In this way the worm will be unable to use its pincers—which, although small, are capable of inflicting quite a sharp nip.

The hook is then inserted in the mouth, and the worm eased around the bend and up the shank before the hook-point is allowed to emerge again, leaving an inch or so of tail dangling. A fine-wire, round-bend hook is best for this, and it should be needle-sharp and free from rust.

Ragworm may be kept in a little gritty sea-damp sand (not mud); among damp seaweed; or between layers of clean sacking damped in *sea* water. Inspect them daily, and remove any dead or ailing worms.

Razorfish. These long bivalve shellfish burrow in gently shelving expanses of sand or slightly muddy sand, near and beyond the limits of low tides. They are a favourite bait of bass anglers when surf fishing, and are also very useful for plaice, dabs, flounders and rays.

A keyhole-shaped depression in the sand marks the entrance to the razorfish's burrow. This should be approached cautiously, for if the shellfish feels the vibration of your footsteps it will immediately shoot downwards—at the same time sending up a tell-tale spurt of water.

There are various methods of collecting razorfish. The hard way is to dig them out. The easy way is to spear them.

Various types of spear are used for this purpose, but an efficient tool can be made from a 30 in. mild steel rod, from 3/16 in. to ¼ in. in diameter. At one end make a loop to serve as a hand-grip. The other end should be heated red-hot, and then beaten out flat. Shape this flattened part to a point on an emery wheel; then cut in some barbs with a hacksaw. Finally, heat the spearhead again, and plunge it into water.

To use the spear, insert it for a few inches into the razorfish's hole, ease it around gently to find the 'run' of the burrow, and then thrust downwards until you feel it enter the razorfish. Drive it well home, twist the spear slightly to set the barbs securely, and then withdraw the razorfish gently and steadily.

Sandeels are a deadly bait for many species of sea fish, including bass, turbot, and big deep-sea pollack. Unfortunately, they are somewhat limited in their distribution, and inshore they are found mainly around bays and estuaries where there is a good run of sand between the tide lines.

It is by digging or scratching in the sand near the limits of the lowest tides that most amateur bait gatherers obtain their sandeels. In some places two kinds are found: the lesser sandeel, which is usually about three to six inches

Baits

long; and the greater sandeel, or cock launce, which may measure ten inches or more in length.

For most kinds of fishing the lesser sandeel is the better bait, and fortunately it also seems to be the more plentiful.

In some areas sandeels lying buried in the sand can be uncovered by quick scooping movements with a digging fork, the sand being flung aside rather than dug over. On the west coast of Ireland, and elsewhere, the favourite tool is an old reaping hook with a notched and blunted blade —the blade being drawn through the sand so that the sandeels are hooked up to the surface.

Sometimes it is necessary to do this in shallow water, such as an estuary tide-pool. Then one needs to be very quick at grabbing the uncovered eels with the other hand, and a beginner will certainly lose many more than he catches.

To overcome this difficulty it is possible to use a sort of rake, with prawn netting stretched over a framework immediately behind it to catch the sandeels as they are fished out. The teeth of the rake are 6 in. nails driven at 4 in. intervals through a wedge-shaped block of wood, and they should be slanted forwards at a fairly sharp angle. (See Fig. 38).

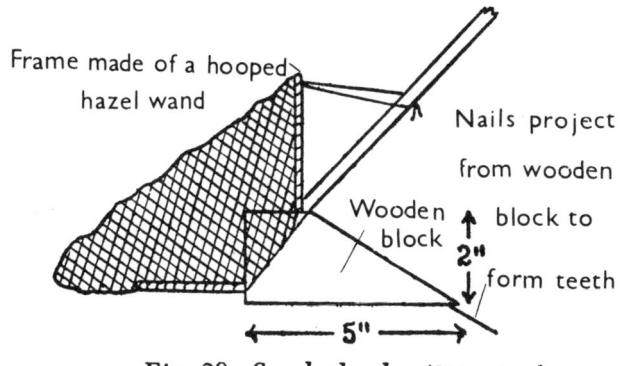

Fig. 38. Sandeel rake. (Side view)

Scraping for sandeels is often most rewarding at night. Moonlight seems to affect them, and on the west coast of

Ireland I have seen remarkable catches made at low tide during the full moon springs.

Whichever method you use to catch your sandeels—or even if you buy them from a professional, it is essential to treat them very carefully if you wish to use them alive. On no account should they be placed in a metal container as this will soon kill them. The best thing to keep them in is a wooden courge, floating at a mooring or behind your boat.

If this is not possible, there is a reasonable chance of keeping sandeels alive for most of the day if placed *immediately* between layers of clean, sea-damped sacking. The life of the sandeels will be prolonged if every so often the sacking is dipped afresh into the sea.

There are several ways of baiting up with sandeels. When driftlining for bass, a common method is to pass the entire hook in through the sandeel's mouth and out through one of its gill openings, and then thrust the point of the hook once only through the underside immediately behind the pectoral fins.

A snag with this method is the limit it imposes on the size of the hook, which must be smaller than the sandeel's mouth and gill opening.

While bearing in mind that too large a hook will spoil the natural swimming action of a sandeel, conditions do sometimes make it advisable to fish with a hook somewhat larger than can be used with the method just described. One useful alternative, especially for trolling, is to hitch a size 10 hook on to the trace just above the main hook. The sandeel is then lip-hooked with the size 10 hook, and the larger one is passed through the underside in the same way as the previous method.

For float fishing, on the other hand, many anglers prefer to pass a single hook thrugh the sandeel's back, near the front of the dorsal fin.

Although it is best to use live sandeels whenever possible, dead or frozen ones are useful, especially if some movement is imparted to them. When driftlining, use sink and draw tactics, and a long trace that wavers attractively

Baits

in the flow of tide. When ground fishing from the shore, retrieve slowly, but twitch the rod tip now and then to make the sandeel give a lifelike dart and flicker.

Shrimps can be caught along many sandy stretches of coast in the low-tide shallows and pools, using a wooden-boomed push-net. They can be kept alive in a floating courge, or amongst wet seaweed.

Live shrimps are a good float fishing bait for inshore pollack, flounders, and peeled raw shrimps are useful for grey mullet.

Ray's Liver. After cutting off the edible wings of thornback rays, do not forget to remove the liver before throwing the carcase to the gulls. This can be a very killing bait for bass, bream, pouting and other species; and small pieces are also taken by grey mullet.

However, owing to its softness, this bait is most suitable for lowering gently into the water from a boat, or driftlining from a jetty.

Snails. Shelled garden snails may be used to catch pouting, wrasse, bream and whiting.

Sprats are netted in autumn and winter around many parts of the coast, and they then make a first-class bait for bass, skate, conger, dogfish, whiting, cod, pollack, turbot, etc. When fishing for whiting, the sprats are usually divided into 'cutlets' after removing the head and tail. For larger species, however, they are generally used whole, except for the possible removal of head and tail. When shore casting it may be necessary to tie whole sprats on to the hook with wool. This applies particularly to shop-bought sprats, which tend to go soft after being packed into boxes.

Squid and Cuttlefish. These are firm baits which stay well on the hook when casting, or subjected to the surge and backscour of heavy surf. A whole squid head is an excellent bait for big conger, and large strips of squid are also first class for sizable bass, cod, skate, etc. Smaller fish will take pieces of squid tentacle. Cuttlefish is also very useful, although not quite so good as squid.

In some areas seaside tackle dealers sell deep-frozen

squid and cuttle, and this is usually one of the most popular baits with the local anglers.

The flesh and tentacles can also be salted down in airtight glass jars. This does not result in such a good bait as deep-freezing, but it makes a very useful standby for the winter months. Some anglers recommend soaking these salted baits in pilchard oil before use.

Freshly caught squid and cuttle can often be obtained from professional fishermen; while sometimes large numbers will attack the boat angler's baited hook with their parrot-like beaks. They will follow the bait to the surface, and may then be caught—sometimes several at a time—in the landing net. Before lifting them aboard, they should be given time to eject their ink.

DEEP-FROZEN BAITS

A few of the baits listed in this chapter can be stored very successfully in a domestic deep-freezer. Among the most useful are sandeels, razorfish and squid. It is essential, of course, to freeze them down as soon as possible after they have been caught.

In late summer I also freeze down plenty of mackerel for use during the winter months. Although freezing tends to soften mackerel flesh, making it a second-rate hook bait, I nevertheless find frozen mackerel extremely useful for mincing up as groundbait when winter fishing for whiting and cod.

It is advisable to freeze all baits in airtight polythene bags, with just sufficient bait in each bag for a single fishing session. Before freezing, draw the air out of each bag through a plastic tube; then seal with a wire tie. All baits should be labelled and dated before being placed in the freezer.

Worm baits do not take kindly to freezing.

Index

Anchoring, 62-63
Angler Fish, 86

Baits, 138 et seq.
Bass, 87-91
Beach fishing, 33 et seq.
Billet, see Coalfish
Boat fishing, 58 et seq.
Boulder Eels, 138
Bream, Black, 91-92
Bream, Red, 92-93
Brill, 93

Casting, 36
Coalfish, 93-95
Cockles, 139
Cod, 96-97
Conger, 98-103
Corrosion, Saltwater, 53
Crabs, Peeler and Soft, 147-149

Dab, 103
Deep-frozen baits, 158
Dogfish, Greater Spotted, 104
Dogfish, Lesser Spotted, 103
Dogfish, Spur, 104
Drag-Lining, 82-84
Drift-Fishing, 82-84
Driftline Fishing, 27, 72-74

Drop-nets, 23-24
'Droppen' spoon, 48

Echo-Sounders, 100

Feathering, 84-85
Float Fishing, 24-27, 30-32, 74
Flounder, 105-107
Frozen baits, 158

Gaffing, 41, 68
Garfish, 107-108
Ground-baiting, 75
Gurnards, 108-109

Haddock, 109
Hake, 109
Halibut, 110
Hermit Crab, 139
Herring, 110-111; as bait 139
Hooks, 19-20

Ingram, Alex, 48

John Dory, 111

Knots, 21, 42

Landing nets, 68-69
Leads, 18, 46, 47, 55, 56, 77

Index

Leger tackle, 29, 30, 71-72
Limpets, 139
Lines, 17-18, 35-36
Ling, 111
Lugworms, 140-143
Lures, Spinning, 47 et seq
Lures, Trolling, 77-80

Mackerel, 111-113, as bait 143
Marks, Locating, 63 et seq.
Mevagissey sandeel, 48
Monel metal line, 17
Monkfish, 113-114
Mullet, Grey, 114-117
Mussels, 144-147

Paternoster tackle, 28, 70-71
Paternoster-trot, 29
Pier Fishing, 22 et seq.
Pilchards (as bait), 149
Plaice, 117-118
Playing a fish, 40
Plummet, 66
Pollack, 118-121
Pouting, 121-122, as bait 150
Prawns, 150-152

Ragworms, 152-154
Ray's liver (as bait), 157
'Red Gill' sandeel, 78, 120

Reels, 13-17, 34-35, 36, 44, 74-75
Rock Fishing, 32
Rods, 7-13, 33, 43-44, 74-75

Safety Afloat, 59 et seq.
Saithe, see Coalfish
Sandbag sinker, 37, 38
Sandeels, 154-156
Scad, 122
Sharks, 122-124
Skate and Rays, 124-127
Skate Liver (as bait), 157
Slipper Limpets, 139-140
Snails, 157
Sole, 127-128
Spinning, 43 et seq., 85
Sprats, 157
Squid, 157-158
Sting Ray, 127

Thornback Ray, 125
Tope, 128-131
Trolling, 76-82
Tunny, 131
Turbot, 131-133

Weever, 133-134
Whiting, 134-135
Wire lines, 16-18
Wrasse, 135-137
Wrecks, 67, 68

Printed in Great Britain by Photo-litho-offset by
Cox & Wyman Ltd, London, Fakenham and Reading